PRODUCING YOUR PORTFOLIO

**A guide to performance-based
evidence collection for City and Guilds
NVQ Level 3 TDLB Courses and other
courses for teaching and training
adult learners**

Richard Stakes and Wendy Nicklin

Trentham Books

Stoke on Trent, UK and Sterling, USA

Trentham Books Limited

Westview House	22883 Quicksilver Drive
734 London Road	Sterling
Oakhill	VA 20166-2012
Stoke on Trent	USA
Staffordshire	
England ST4 5NP	

First published 2000

British Library Cataloguing-in-Publication Data
A catalogue record for this book is available from the British Library

1 85856 200 7 (paperback)

Designed and typeset by Trentham Print Design Ltd., Chester and printed in Great Britain by Biddles Ltd., Surrey.

Contents

v

List of Tables

PREFACE

This book is a practical handbook which provides information and guidance for students putting together a portfolio of evidence to qualify for various awards for teaching or training adult learners.

The authors are both experienced assessors and verifiers for these awards, and have considerable experience of providing guidance and advice to candidates. In our experience there are two major areas of concern for candidates. One is interpreting the requirements set out in the standards; the other is providing the evidence required to meet the standards for each unit.

The main awards the book will concentrate on are:

City and Guilds 7306 award for Teaching and Training Adults

City and Guilds 7281 award for Training and Development

City and Guilds 7231 award for Learning Support Assistants (level 02)

Foundation teaching award

The book is also a suitable reference book for those who are putting together 'mini awards' composed of various units, including the **D32** and **D33 Assessor Awards**.

Since a number of different awards can be achieved by combining units described in this book, the work required to achieve competence in each unit has been described in full. Although this leads to some repetition, this is a deliberate policy which ensures that each unit is a coherent whole. However, where there is an overlap in the evidence presented in a portfolio, students should follow the advice set out by City and Guilds in their candidate packs and cross-reference evidence across a range of units.

Chapter 1 focuses on the terminology of National Vocational Qualifications (NVQs). These awards use jargon of their own, which is sometimes difficult to penetrate. Particular attention will be given in this chapter to the concept of an NVQ. This will be done by discussing a series of questions we are commonly asked. The most common of these relate to the assessment procedure. What is an NVQ? What is meant by 'producing and collecting evidence' for an NVQ award? What is a portfolio, what should it contain and how do I best organise it?

Chapter 2 provides an overview of the teaching process, based on a commonly used five-point approach which relates to the planning, presentation and evaluation of teaching sessions. This approach also links to the titles of the units that make up the various awards covered in this book. The chapter gives only a brief introduction to the teaching process, so references are provided to other publications which cover the theoretical underpinning in far more detail. Candidates are strongly advised to refer to these when pursuing evidence to fulfil the requirements listed for underpinning knowledge for each unit.

Chapters 3–7 look at the requirements of the standards. Each chapter uses the same format to provide a uniformity of approach. Chapter 3 explains how to collect evidence which shows your knowledge of the development needs of your learners. Chapter 4 is about evidence relating to the preparation of teaching sessions. Chapter 5 deals with the presentation of sessions and Chapter 6 with the collection of assessment information about your learners. Chapter 7 is about collecting evidence of your skills at personal professional evaluation.

Each chapter has an introductory section describing its content. The second section describes the unit requirements in detail and provides practical examples of the evidence required. The third section looks at some of the underpinning knowledge requirements for the unit. Each chapter ends with case studies, based on real life examples, showing how candidates put together their evidence for the unit.

CHAPTER ONE

THE CONCEPT OF VOCATIONAL QUALIFICATIONS

Introduction

To help you build your portfolio this chapter discusses some of the key concepts underlying National Vocational Qualifications (NVQs). It looks at a number of commonly asked questions, including:

- What is an NVQ and how does it work in practice?

- How are NVQs assessed?

- What is meant by evidence in the context of NVQs?

- What is a portfolio?

- What does action-planning mean?

- How should I organise my portfolio?

- How can I obtain witness statements or testimonials?

- What is cross-referencing and how do I do it?

The chapter ends with twelve key questions you should ask yourself before presenting your portfolio for assessment.

National Vocational Qualifications

National Vocational Qualifications (NVQs) are designed to identify and accredit people's competence to perform work-related activities to set standards. (In Scotland these awards are called Scottish Vocational Qualification (SVQs). To simplify matters, we will refer to both awards as NVQs. Over the past decade NVQs have been developed by specialists from leading groups within a particular industry or sector in order to make vocational education more responsive to the needs of industry and to create a more appropriate range of awards. The awards are approved by the Qualifications and Curriculum Authority (QCA) and are based on agreed **occupational standards** intended to meet employers' needs at different performance levels within the workforce.

2

NVQ LEVELS

Level I: Foundation and basic work activities
Competence in the performance of a range of varied work activities, most of which may be routine and predictable

Level 2: A broad range of skills and responsibilities
More demanding range of varied work activities, performed in a variety of contexts. At this level some of the activities are complex or non-routine and there is some individual responsibility. Working with others may often be necessary

Level 3: Complex skilled and or supervisory work
At this level learners will have a broad range of varied skilled activities, many of which are complex and non-routine, and performed in a wide variety of contexts. At Level 3 there is considerable individual responsibility, often with guidance and supervision of others.

Level 4: Managerial/Specialist
Broad range of complex specialised, technical and professional activities. At Level 4 there is a substantial amount of personal responsibility and responsibility of others.

Level 5: Professional/Senior Managerial
With Level 5 workloads there is a substantial level of personal accountability and autonomy. At this level learners will have a significant responsibility for the work of others and for the allocation of resources, accountability for analysis and diagnosis, design, planning, execution and evaluation.

Figure 1: A comparison between NVQ award levels and more traditional qualifications

---

NVQs cover five levels of responsibility, ranging from level 1 (work described as basic) to level 5 (complex work with high levels of responsibility). Figure 1 provides details of each level.

The main focus of NVQ awards is on ensuring a suitable level of performance, to meet prescribed criteria. Knowledge, skills and understanding are relevant to the performance of activities.

The emphasis on personal performance (or competence) demanded by NVQs contrasts sharply with many previous vocational and professional qualifications, where the emphasis was on testing knowledge. Although many people may require training to reach NVQ standards, these awards are not training programmes, nor are they linked to any particular training programme.

NVQ awards were first introduced in 1988 and were based mainly on assessments carried out in the workplace on specific skills often associated with particular jobs. More recently however there have been two important changes to the system: increased compatibility amongst the various awards, to allow candidates more flexibility in using their different abilities and aptitudes; and a greater reliance on work-placed assessment. The model for the development of a new NVQ is shown in figure 2.

3

National Training Organisations define occupational standards

Awarding bodies consider customer need and make application to QCA/SQCA

Standards approved by QCA/SQCA

Award recognised and implemented by awarding body

Award offered to centres

Programme reviewed, evaluated and updated, where necessary

Figure 2: The development of a new NVQ/SVQ award

The 7306 award relates to teaching; the 7281 award the focuses on training and development; and the 7321 award is concerned with the role of the learning support assistant (LSA). NVQs based on occupational standards are composed of **units** that describe a particular aspect of the work. Each unit is made up of several **elements**. These are defined by **Performance Criteria** (PCs), **Range Statements** and **Underpinning Knowledge**. These are described as areas of competence. These areas of competence define the standards and detail the required level of performance and knowledge required at the different levels of responsibility described in Figure 1.

Assessing NVQs

The assessment process consists of three stages:

- **planning** what you have to do to meet the standards

- **collecting evidence** of your competence and judging it against the standards

- **receiving feedback** from your assessor and, where necessary, agreeing a time for further assessment.

To gain an award, competence against the national standards must be demonstrated to a qualified assessor appointed by an approved centre. When the assessor is satisfied that the candidate is competent and the decision has been verified, the appropriate awarding body will award a certificate.

What is meant by evidence?

Work-related activities, observed by your assessor, are the best source of evidence. However, with the awards that are the focus of this book this is sometimes unrealistic, particularly where a large number of units is involved and complex activities have to be performed. In such circumstances, there are other ways you may be able to use to demonstrate your competence, for example:

- Performing a **simulation** of your work

- Presenting a **product** arising from your work

- Undertaking a **written assignment**

4

- Providing a **supplementary statement**

- Answering **questions** set by your assessor for professional discussion

- Presenting a **witness statement** from a colleague or someone you teach, describing your performance.

At NVQ Levels 1 and 2, the evidence presented for assessment will typically be the result of observations made by an assessor in the work place and recorded in a logbook. This logbook will have space to write down the activities observed. These are then 'signed off' by both assessor and candidate. If candidates have other evidence of competent performance, such as evidence of previous qualifications or experience, this can be attached to the logbook. This type of evidence from past experience is sometimes called **APL (Accreditation of Prior Learning)**.

At NVQ Levels 3, 4 and 5 (the levels at which you are working) direct observation is not always possible or appropriate. Here it may be more suitable that evidence is presented in the form of reports, designs, judgements made by other people and certificates. This mixture of evidence from a variety of sources is called **diverse evidence**. Typically, diverse evidence is gathered together into a portfolio.

5

What is a portfolio?

A portfolio is a collection of documentary evidence from diverse sources. In some ways this is similar to portfolios produced by architects, photographic models and artists when they are tendering for work, trying to gain employment or seeking funding: a collection of evidence demonstrating professional competence over a period of time. Similarly, portfolios for these awards should demonstrate your professional competence.

In the case of the architect tendering for work from a company, the portfolio will be judged against the company's opinion of the qualities required for the job; but in the case of an NVQ portfolio the assessor will judge your evidence against the national standards described above. The assessor can only accept the evidence if it meets the standards laid down for the relevant units of the award.

What should be in my portfolio?

Your portfolio should contain the evidence that proves you are competent in relation to the standards of all the NVQ units you are taking. Portfolios are commonly set out in ring binders or box files. You are advised to keep your evidence collection to a minimum. This will make the process easier for you to deal with, and for your assessor to evaluate.

Rules of evidence

The rules of evidence help an assessor to make judgements about your evidence. When looking at your portfolio, the assessor will be asking 'What does this evidence tell me?' They will be checking your portfolio using what are described as the rules of evidence. These rules relate to the validity, authenticity, currency and sufficiency of your evidence. Here is a brief explanation of each of these rules as it affects the assessment of NVQs

- **Validity.** Does the evidence relate to the specified standards set out in the units? Remember that evidence may be relevant to some or all of the elements and/or the range statements.

- **Authenticity.** This rule relates to how the assessor knows that the evidence is really yours. The assessor will want to be sure that the evidence contained in the portfolio presents an accurate and true reflection of your own activities and competence.

- **Currency.** The assessor has to be satisfied that the evidence shows your current competence in the units or elements you have presented for assessment and will be making sure that the skills you have demonstrated continue to be current practice. This is particularly important with historical evidence. The assessor will examine whether the equipment, work practices or regulations have changed since the evidence was produced, and will be looking for evidence that you continue to retain any competence that was demonstrated at some time in the past.

- **Sufficiency.** In this area your assessor will be looking to see if there is enough evidence of the right quality to demonstrate

6

consistent competence. They will wish to be confident about the degree to which evidence of performance covers the different contexts (range statements) specified in the standards.

The assessor will also be making sure there is evidence of your ability to consistently perform the tasks described in each of the units of your award. It is important to bear in mind that having a lot of evidence does not guarantee it is the right evidence.

In the context of the NVQ approach, it is important to be aware that an assessment of competence is designed to be open and accessible to all those involved and that an assessor is not trying to trip you up or catch you out.

Cross-referencing evidence

Covering all the units in an award does not mean that you require a separate individual piece of evidence for each element: evidence you have used for one unit may be used again for another. Remember it's the quality of evidence that counts, not the quantity!

7

You must gather enough evidence to satisfy the rules of evidence without the process developing into a paper chase, making your portfolio unmanageable for both yourself and your assessor. It is not necessary to go for 'over-kill'. You should try to re-use cross-reference evidence across units and elements wherever appropriate and not photocopy the same evidence unnecessarily. This is described as cross-referencing evidence. Where a piece of evidence is cross-referenced you should quote its unique evidence reference code in an index of the evidence you have collected.

Sources of Evidence

Evidence comes from four sources: **direct performance evidence, indirect performance evidence, supplementary evidence** and **historical evidence**.

Direct performance evidence

Direct performance evidence (also called **primary evidence**) is most commonly collected by your assessor observing you in your place of work. There are two main sources of this type of evidence:

- **observation by your assessor,** in this form of assessment notes describing what was observed and how the performance criteria and range requirements were met for each of the units observed are made

- **products of your performance at work,** for example letters, memos or reports produced during the course of work; items such as handouts, overhead projector sheets, computer print-outs, photographs or videos of the products themselves; or examples of your learner's work

Indirect performance evidence

Indirect performance evidence can be obtained through the comments and testimonials of others who know about your teaching skills but who, unlike your assessor, do not formally observe you. Such people include your line manager, other colleagues with whom you teach and your learners. These people may be able to provide you with either oral or written confirmation of your skills. It is important to remember that this evidence must relate directly to the standards set out for the award.

This evidence may be drawn from a variety of sources, including letters, reports and appraisals. These are sometimes referred to as **witness statements** or endorsements. Other indirect performance evidence includes personal certificates, personal reports about your own teaching, reflections on your personal performance, projects you have completed, role-plays and case studies. Your assessor or adviser may suggest a project, assignment, or simulation of your work in order to supplement the evidence and ensure coverage of the standards.

Supplementary evidence

Supplementary evidence can be collected from records of interviews with your assessor. Their assessment of your evidence and any supplementary questions they have asked you are common examples of this form of evidence. A less common example for the awards detailed in this book would be a knowledge test demonstrating your underpinning knowledge of the standards.

Historical evidence

If you had some experience of teaching before taking this award some of your teaching activities may be useful as evidence. However, they must meet two criteria to be valid evidence. Firstly, they must be relevant to the unit or element you are claiming and secondly, they must continue to apply to your current practice.

Witnesses, testimonies and endorsements

A number of different people may be involved with your assessment. These people play a role in observing your activities and so may support your claim to competence. It is the assessor's responsibility to judge the value of other people's observations.

Your colleagues and managers as well as your learners may witness particular activities that take place during or shortly before your evidence gathering-stage. These people are sometimes called **witnesses** or **observers.** The activities may involve paid or unpaid work but must all relate to the standards.

Your assessor will usually observe a proportion of your performance. The observations of other witnesses may provide you with evidence of your consistency and your ability to repeat activities competently.

Witnesses may simply confirm that a particular piece of work was done by you by signing, dating and/or making a statement at the bottom of the work, or they may offer a written account of your performance. Such accounts are often called **testimonies** or **endorsements.** These statements are of most relevance if the witness is fully aware of what you want them to confirm and of the standards being targeted. You have a responsibility to ensure that your witnesses are fully informed.

In order to help those who are providing you with witness statements you should:

- explain why the witness testimony is required

9

- provide the witness with a copy of the relevant standards

- explain the specific experience, activity or task you are doing in relation to the specific performance criteria

- explain the particular activity in relation to the specific range statement

- encourage the witness to provide their statement on letter-headed paper.

As with the rest of your evidence, witness statements should be given an appropriate reference code and placed with the rest of your evidence in your portfolio.

For such witness information to be meaningful, you should list all those people involved with any aspect of the assessment process. This will help anyone assessing your portfolio to understand each person's role in the evidence collection and assessment process. In their candidate pack, City and Guilds, for example, have provided a pro forma for this activity. This information should be placed near the beginning of the portfolio.

10

Action Planning

In planning the evidence collection for your award you should spend some time thinking about what you need to put into your portfolio and how to set it out. This process is called **action planning**. An example of an action plan is shown in Figure 3.

Action plans are important in tracking the assessment process through the award process. Both you and your assessor should retain copies of these documents. They may be needed for **verification** (a check on overall quality of the assessment) by either the internal or the external verifier.

In addition to such evidence, there should be some basic information showing your breadth of experience, so that a verifier can understand the context in which the evidence presented.

Action Plan

Name ————————————

Unit Title ———————————————— Element Title ————————————————

Performance Criteria (pc)	Evidence I already have to meet the requirements of this pc	Evidence that I need to find to meet the requirements of this pc	Evidence that I need to think about to meet the requirements of this pc
A			
B			
C			
D			
E			
Etc.			

Figure 3: A typical action plan

Criteria for a good portfolio

11

The assessment process is much easier if your evidence is presented in an organised manner that assists both you and the assessor to relate it to the standards. You should try to ensure that the portfolio is easy to follow and that the competences you are claiming can easily be matched with the relevant evidence. You must decide whether to present the evidence in clusters based on units or elements or to place all the documentation at the front with a single evidence section at the back of the portfolio. You may have some freedom of choice here but your assessor will advise you, perhaps indicating, in their experience, which is the best and simplest way to organise your evidence.

Your aim should be to produce a portfolio that:

- provides a clear structure for people to follow
- cross-references each piece of evidence with the appropriate standards
- contains all the evidence for the units you are taking, or reference to any evidence you are presenting for assessment that is not contained in the portfolio (including its location).

Whichever method you choose you will also need to provide a rationale for each unit. This rationale should provide a summary of how you obtained your evidence indicating how it relates to your teaching and the NVQ standards. Either a unit or an element summary may be used; normally it is sufficient to produce a rationale for each unit, but you will need to negotiate this with your assessor.

Information to be included for unit

For each unit you want assessed you should include the following information:

- **A copy of the standards and assessment guidance for elements.** Including the standards usually helps the candidate to keep focused on the award and can help the assessor in judging the evidence.

- **A unit summary of evidence document.** This provides a description of the evidence, indicating which parts of the unit or elements are covered by a particular piece of evidence, and where this may be found.

- **A rationale for each unit.** This rationale is an explanation of your reasons for including the evidence that you have selected. Each rationale should be a clear and unambiguous statement of the purpose of the evidence you have presented, in what context it was used and from what source of your teaching experience it was drawn. Your reasons for including particular pieces of evidence will vary from one unit to another: it may demonstrate something that is typical of your performance, or a particular aspect of your skill or work you are currently undertaking. If you are presenting a number of units it may be useful to include a **curriculum vitae** (CV) in your portfolio. This will not only detail your career profile but can also be used to provide useful information about your current teaching responsibilities.

- **Your evidence.** This should include all your evidence for each unit or element you want assessed along with a unique reference code for each page you have included. Do not worry

12

Fig 4: An example of a summary of evidence grid

CITY AND GUILDS 7306/7281

SUMMARY OF EVIDENCE GRID

UNIT NO: _____ UNIT TITLE _____

ELEMENT NO: _____ ELEMENT TITLE _____

Evidence No:																								
P.C.s																								
a																								
b																								
c																								
d																								
e																								
f																								
g																								
h																								
I																								
j																								
k																								
Range																								
1																								
2																								
3																								
4																								
5																								
6																								
7																								
8																								
Knowledge																								
1																								
2																								
3																								
4																								
5																								
6																								
7																								
8																								
9																								
10																								
11																								
12																								
13																								

The evidence for this element has been reviewed. The evidence is valid, sufficient and an authentic record of the candidate's current competence with relation to the standards.

Candidate's signature _____ ·Date _____

Assessor's signature _____ Date_____

13

too much about the order of your evidence pages, as there are no requirements laid down by the awarding body about this. You can collect your evidence together, number it in any order and then cross reference it in the **unit summary of evidence** document described above.

- **A summary of evidence grid.** This evidence grid will serve to show that you have covered all the requirements listed in each elements. An example of one approach using a 'tick box' on a generic grid is shown in Figure 4. The generic grid has sufficient space in each of the evidence areas for it to be used flexibly for any of the units in your award.

The assessment procedure

It is possible that three people will assess your portfolio at some stage. Your assessor will of course have the greatest influence on it. It is your assessor who has the responsibility of ensuring that the guidelines set out by City and Guilds have been followed, the evidence you have produced is appropriate, you have completed an assessment plan for each unit, and you have been fully informed about the assessment process.

14

Both the internal and the external verifiers, as guardians of the standards set by the awarding body, examine portfolios in order to check the quality of the assessment made by the assessor. This also ensures that the work being undertaken by your assessor is being completed satisfactorily.

You should bear in mind the date agreed for submitting your portfolio to your assessor. It is important to work towards this date and to maintain the momentum of evidence collection. However, if unforeseen problems arise and you are unable to meet your deadline, you should negotiate a new date for submission with your assessor. In such circumstances all your action plans and schedules should be amended appropriately.

When reviewing your portfolio the assessor will be looking for evidence of performance meeting the standards sufficiently to encourage confidence in your ability to carry out the work described in the element and unit titles. The assessor will be using the NVQ **rules of evidence**.

In the context of the NVQ approach, it is important to be aware that an assessment of competence is designed to be transparent to all those involved and that an assessor is not trying to trip you up or catch you out.

Questions you should consider when presenting your portfolio for assessment

Before presenting your portfolio for assessment it may be useful to consider the following questions as a checklist:

1 Is there sufficient evidence to cover all the performance criteria?

2 Does your evidence enable an assessor to make judgements about how you can operate in a range of settings?

3 Does the evidence satisfy the specific assessment requirements of each element or unit?

4 Is the evidence relevant to the element or elements of competence claimed?

5 Is the evidence still current? Does it show how the standards are met now?

6 Is the evidence clearly your own work? Is it clearly linked to your performance and not that of others?

7 Is the evidence true? Can it be confirmed that it is real and not made up?

8 Is there enough evidence drawn from a variety of sources?

9 If asked, could you explain the reason for producing each of the various pieces of evidence?

10 Is the portfolio presented so that an assessor, even one with little knowledge of your role, can easily follow the evidence and see how it justifies your claim of competence?

11 Have you demonstrated your underpinning knowledge for the units for which you are being assessed? Have you shown that you have done some reading about the topic?

Summary

This chapter has introduced you to NVQs and described some important concepts for those who are undertaking any of the City and Guilds Level 3 awards. It has included information central to an understanding of the purposes of NVQs, and their organisation, assessment and language, in order to help you in your thinking about developing your own portfolio of evidence.

16

CHAPTER TWO

THE PROCESS OF TEACHING

Introduction

This chapter provides an overview of the professional skills and knowledge required for organising and managing teaching and training sessions successfully. It is based on a five-point model of teaching relating to good classroom practice. These five separate yet closely interlinked activities are

- identifying individual learners' needs

- planning teaching or training sessions

- classroom management

- the assessment of learners

- professional evaluation.

The five-point model forms the basis of the evidence requirements set out in the units of competence for the City and Guilds teaching and training awards.

Overview

It has been argued by many concerned with teaching and training adults (eg. Daines et al., 1993, Walkin, 1990, Kerry et al., 1992 and Curzon, 1993) that, in order to be a successful teacher, there are five key areas to be taken into consideration.

These areas fall into two broad categories relating to developing professional relationships with learners and the process of managing and organising teaching and learning. The former category relates to the acquisition of interpersonal skills with learners and the development of an appropriate working relationship them. The second category concentrates on the mechanics of classroom management: the planning, delivery, assessment and evaluation of lessons.

It has been argued by Reece and Walker (1992, p.8) that the teaching process is linear, however others (eg. Stakes and Hornsby, 1996) have pointed out that it is a cyclical operation, a continuous process that continues from one teaching session to another. This process is illustrated in Figure 5.

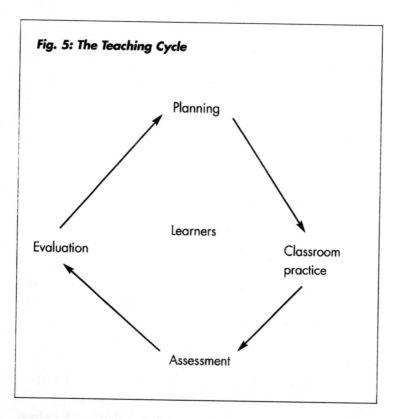

Fig. 5: The Teaching Cycle

Planning

Learners

Evaluation

Classroom practice

Assessment

The diagram above is, of course, far too simplistic to be of great practical value, as each stage is built up out of a number of component parts. The Further Education National Training Organisation (FENTO, 1999) demonstrated some of the complexities involved in these areas. In this document they present a set of standards based on a model of seven key areas of competence for

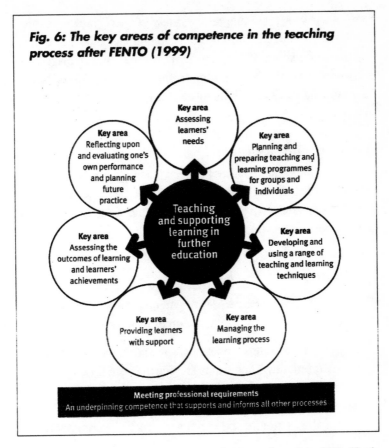

Fig. 6: The key areas of competence in the teaching process after FENTO (1999)

teaching and supporting learners in further education (FE). Each of these key areas, as illustrated in Figure 6, is sub-divided into areas of generic knowledge that display the real complexity of the teaching process.

The complexity shown in Figure 6 is forcefully confirmed by the demands made in any of the candidate packs for the TDLB awards. The professional demands made on teachers and trainers are complicated, even confusing, demanding not only that they have a detailed knowledge of each of these areas and a sound knowledge of their particular subject area, but also that they can demonstrate these in the practical situation.

It is not the purpose of this book to discuss these skills in any great detail. This has been done elsewhere by Walkin, Kerry et al., Curzon, and Reece and Walker among others. However, from the point of view of providing an overview of the competences detailed in the awards, it is useful to use the model shown in Figure 6 to illustrate some of the key organisational and management skills needed by teachers and trainers. The activities described in the following sections will be discussed in much greater detail in subsequent chapters.

Working with learners

There is an important balance between teaching as an activity and the process of learning, and the needs of the learner should be the central consideration of your thinking and planning. Some important considerations are:

- your knowledge of the appropriateness of the programme you teach, and any suitable alternatives to it

- possible lines of career development for your learners, and any suitable courses or other sources of information

- basic rules of human relationships and classroom management techniques. These rules include the need for consistency, fairness, approachability honesty, knowledge of their personal needs and handling relationships effectively, as well as issues of equal opportunity and racial and gender discrimination.

Planning

Planning involves setting both the aims of the course of study and the objectives for each session. The aims will may remain constant (teaching someone a certain skill or developing their knowledge of a process), but the objectives set for each session may vary. Variations may arise as you develop a better knowledge of your learners and their individual needs. At the planning stage you need to make sure that your subject knowledge is adequate for each session you teach and that you are prepared for any questions your learners may ask you.

Your lesson plans need to be thought out in a systematic and clear way and should include details of any resources you might need. At this stage you will also need to consider your method of delivery. You might choose the **traditional** role of a giver of information, the didactic teacher directing from the front of the class and providing information for others to learn. You might choose instead the role of the teacher as **facilitator**, assisting learners and producing individual programmes for them with different and varied tasks. A third, and very common alternative, is to mix and match the roles described above.

• Classroom practice

Classroom practice encompasses delivering what you have planned, and managing your learners. Some important questions about this part of your role include:

- What are your strategies for creating a positive atmosphere in the room where you work, and how do you put your learners at ease?

- What method of delivery and which resources will you use?

- How will you ensure that the level of the work is appropriate for your learners and that it is correctly paced for effective learning?

- How will you set appropriate tasks for your learners both to reinforce your teaching and to improve their confidence in their developing knowledge and skill?

- How will you deal with awkward situations and respond flexibly to unforeseen events?

- How will you ensure that you meet national legislative requirements such as those relating to equal opportunities and health and safety?

• Assessment

When assessing your learners, you need to ensure that the tasks you set match what you have taught them and the objectives you have set. These objectives may be set out as targets that your learners have to meet.

You will need to consider whether to use a **formative** or **summative** form of assessment. The term **formative assessment** refers to assessments taken as part of the teaching process: feedback from learners is used to identify their current difficulties and work on them. **Summative assessment** refers to assessments taken at the end of a course or a phase of learning.

Beyond this, you will also have to decide if you will use an **informal** approach (questions round the group at the beginning or end of sessions) or a **formal** approach (the 'pencil and paper' approach) when checking what has been learned. With a formal test you may also need to know if it is **criterion-referenced** (set against standards which have to be attained, eg. the driving test) or **norm-referenced** (set against standardised norms).

As part of the process of assessment it is also important to bear in mind that your learners will need feedback, and you should not only check their work promptly but also try to ensure that there is a balance in your feedback between negative and positive comments.

• Evaluation

22

Whereas the assessment process focuses on the learner, evaluation focuses on you and the development of your professional skills. The TDLB awards concentrate on two aspects of this: the evaluation of your personal performance, and the quality of your teaching. Key questions you might ask here include:

- Were the aims of your sessions met?

- Did you have appropriate resources?

- How successful were your teaching aids?

- Were classroom relationships good?

- Was your assessment strategy appropriate, and did you assess what you had taught?

- What judgement can you make about your learners' behaviour?

The second area of concern is evaluating your professional needs. Key questions here include:

- Are you keeping up to date with your subject knowledge?

- Are you aware of changes and developments in your subject area

- Are you aware of national changes affecting educational provision in the sector in which you teach?

Summary

This chapter, through a simple, commonly used teaching model, has provided an introduction the professional skills of the teacher or trainer. This model, based on the cycle of session planning, classroom organisation and management, learner assessment and personal evaluation, is closely identified with the model used in the City and Guilds 7306/7281 courses. As such, this chapter serves as an appropriate basis for the information given in subsequent chapters of this book, which explain approaches that will help you to build a portfolio of evidence of your teaching competence.

23

CHAPTER THREE

The A Units
Knowing your learners' needs

Introduction

The City and Guilds A units focus on identifying the needs of those you teach or train. At NVQ Level 3 there is only one unit, A22 Identify individual learners' needs. This unit requires you to provide evidence of your skills in the following activities:

- Assessing the individual needs of all your learners, including those with learning difficulties, physical disabilities and differences in aptitude and ability,

25

- Collecting and evaluating information about learners' previous experiences and qualifications

- Agreeing individual learning programmes

- Accrediting learners' prior experience and learning

- Conducting initial assessments with learners

- Using the methods and techniques of training needs analysis for your learners

PORTFOLIO REQUIREMENTS

A22: Identify individual learners' needs

Unit A22 is concerned firstly with collecting evidence to demonstrate your knowledge and level of competence in identifying the needs and aspirations of your learners; and secondly with offering a suitable teaching programme for them. The unit looks at a number of the activities involved in the initial assessment of learners, including:

- interviewing learners to establish their current level of qualification and skill

- gathering precise information on their training or learning needs

- identifying a range of possible learning options or programmes from which they can choose

- matching these programmes with their needs and requirements

Performance Criteria

To meet the requirements of this unit your evidence must show how you were able to:

- interview learners successfully about their perceived learning needs and provide them with a needs analysis,

26
- identify and agree their level of current competence

- undertake their initial assessment through the use of witness statements, work-placed assessment or formal or informal testing procedures,

- provide information about any system that may allow them to claim credit for prior experience and learning

- help them to prioritise their learning needs

- advise them of suitable programmes of learning available both within your organisation and outside it

- recommend, or where appropriate adapt or design, programmes to meet their individual needs

Examples of the evidence you could find useful to demonstrate your awareness of the range and purpose of suitable courses for your learners might include:

- information on the purpose of courses they are considering taking, and the level of qualification and method of assessment. This can be drawn from a wide range of material including course prospectuses, brochures, leaflets, display posters and flyers as well as promotional videos, photographs of exhibition displays and press advertisements

- the duration of courses

- the organisation of courses. For example, are they part-time or full-time, where and when does the teaching takes place and what is the length of individual sessions?

In your portfolio you also need to demonstrate your awareness not only of the features and outcomes of the course(s) you teach, but also of other suitable courses available for learners in your area, either at your own place of work or at other local establishments. You should also be able to demonstrate your knowledge of courses your learners might take once they have completed their current studies. Suitable evidence might include literature produced by your place of work, references to visits you have made to other places of work, work-place observations, or liaison with other teachers or supervisors about such courses.

27

It is possible, on some occasions, that learners may wish to transfer to another course they feel is more appropriate to meet their needs. It is important, should this situation arise, that you are able to show that you can provide information on such alternative provision, or indicate who might best be approached.

You should also indicate your ability to provide information about arrangements to help learners attend your course. Evidence you may consider including in your portfolio could cover:

- finance and funding arrangements, bursaries and grants

- the need for a realistic working environment (RWE) for training

- issues relating to equal entitlement and anti-discriminatory practice for learners

Knowledge evidence

The knowledge evidence for this unit requires you to concentrate on two areas

- Identification of suitable learning opportunities for potential learners. This includes knowledge of your programme of work, the time needed to complete it successfully, the intellectual demands the programme makes on learners and the level of attainment or experience required for the course.

- The individual needs of your learners, including knowledge of how they learn best as well as the approach to learning and assessment that your course requires.

Your portfolio will have to show evidence of your knowledge of appropriate interviewing techniques to elicit the information from a variety of learners: for example adults who wish to return to formal learning as well as those who have more recent experience of it. You may also need information about the commitment of your learners and their overall personality and characteristics.

28   Your portfolio should indicate your knowledge of equal opportunities and anti-discriminatory practice. You will need to demonstrate your knowledge of how to work with learners from a variety of social and cultural backgrounds and with a range of attitudes towards learning. Examples may include, on the one hand, learners who show personal timidity, a lack of articulateness or even anxiety, about the course they are considering; and on the other hand, those who are over-confident, even arrogant.

Your knowledge evidence must take into account the short-term needs of your learners as well as their longer-term aspirations, their level of personal motivation, and the importance of balancing these issues with their personal and social circumstances.

You may also need to show your skills at assessing the needs of individuals and interpreting the results of such an assessment. This may include either assessing an individual learner or screening a larger group to determine their level of competence prior to starting a course or training programme. You may also need to have information about sources of additional, more specialist assessment.

Such assessment may need to be interpreted, and you may need to show in your portfolio how you explained, interpreted and presented these results to your learners. Further, you may need to record the information that initial assessments have provided, and your portfolio may be used to present evidence of your skill in this area of your work.

In some cases your learners may come with previous experience, other qualifications or part qualifications they may use towards the award or qualification they are now proposing to seek. In such circumstances you will need to accredit them with this prior experience or learning through the process of Accreditation of Prior Experience and Learning (APEL) set out by the awarding body.

UNDERPINNING KNOWLEDGE

Interviewing learners

Your portfolio should provide evidence of your skills at interviewing learners who are applying for a course or considering their options. You should show that you are aware that interviewing is a two-way process and that a well-organised interview requires you to:

- provide your learners with relevant information

- conduct the session at an appropriate level of vocabulary and sentence construction for them to participate fully

- check on the level of understanding of what you have said

- listen actively

- use a variety of questioning techniques

- agree achievable targets

- arrange further meetings to consider progress and provide support

- maintain confidentiality

- summarise the main points covered

Accreditation of Prior Experience and Learning

An Accreditation of Prior Experience and Learning (APEL) scheme allows a learner to have relevant previous experience and/ or learning recognised and counted towards an NVQ award. For such experience to count it needs to be recent experience, often defined as either current or acquired during the last two years.

Although you may feel that your learners have appropriate experience and will be able to make a claim, this may not be a decision you are able to take on your own. In such a situation you will need to negotiate with an APEL adviser. Similarly, if you feel that your learners have learning acquired less recently that could count towards an award, you will need to discuss this with your adviser.

CASE STUDIES

Here are some case studies of candidates who have successfully presented evidence of competence for this unit. To help you, they are drawn from a variety of teaching and training sources.

Case study 1

Jane, a lecturer in further education runs an enrolment/induction session for prospective catering students before the start of the academic year. She successfully completed this unit with evidence which included:

- course leaflets for two different courses – one for a short part-time course, the other for a one-year full-time course

- relevant pages from the college prospectus

- the induction session programme

- copies of two completed application forms

- information from a questionnaire and from a game played during the first teaching sessions, to identify needs

- results of literacy and numeracy tests taken by two students

- resource lists for the two courses

- case studies of discussions with two students to identify their learning needs and outline how to offer them support

- action plans prepared for two students as a result of discussions (including qualifications, results of tests, school reports and previous experience).

- statements from students confirming the support provided

- financial implications and support available

- a student handbook

Case study 2

Tom, a training co-ordinator, identified learning needs of unemployed adults, and produced the following evidence to complete this unit successfully:

- course leaflets

- a printout from a computer program used to question individuals and identify preferred careers

- a tape recording of advisory interviews with two learners

- results of literacy and numeracy tests

- action plans which identify previous experience, qualifications, training needs and recommended actions

- details of support available for learners, including financial support, childcare, disability support and learning support

- a statement outlining how to identify learning needs and match them to opportunities.

- an account of how equal opportunities and anti-discriminatory practices on the course were followed

REFERENCE TO OTHER TLDB UNITS

The work you have completed for this unit can be linked with the requirements for other TLDB awards, including the following elements:

B221: Identify options for training and development sessions

C211: Create a climate conducive to learning

C222: Agree learning programmes with learners

D36: Advise and support candidates to identify prior achievement

SUMMARY

This chapter has described the type of evidence you need to provide when completing the A unit for the Level 3 award. This evidence relates particularly to meeting the needs and aspirations of your learners.

32

The chapter was also concerned with the background knowledge for successfully interviewing new learners, and with giving them the opportunity to have their previous experience count towards the award they are seeking.

CHAPTER FOUR

The B units Preparation

Introduction

The City and Guilds B units are concerned with the design and preparation of programmes and resources used in the presentation and delivery of teaching sessions. These units assess your ability and skills when interpreting the curriculum needs of your learners, designing programmes for them and preparing resources. In particular they concentrate on your skills in the following areas:

- matching the curriculum with an appropriate programme of learning

- ways of learning and learning strategies

- ways of selecting teaching methods based on suitable learning theory

- the relationship between personal learning styles and the outcomes of learning programmes

- practical approaches to individual and group learning

- approaches to overcoming barriers to learners

At NVQ Level 3 there are two units to be covered in your portfolio. These are B22 Design training and development sessions and B33 Prepare and develop resources to support learners. B22 relates to the design and planning of your teaching or training sessions; B33 is concerned with your skills when preparing and developing resources to aid your teaching.

PORTFOLIO REQUIREMENTS

B22: Design training and development sessions

This unit is concerned with planning the teaching and training sessions you undertake. The main focus is on both the thinking process and the practicalities involved. In particular the unit concentrates on:

- writing aims and objectives for sessions

- selecting appropriate teaching methods

- selecting appropriate resources

The unit comprises two elements: B221, which relates to possible ways of planning teaching sessions, and B222, which concentrates on planning sessions. Your planning should include the style of presentation you will make as well as the resources you will use. Your evidence for this unit must be taken from two different sessions you have taught. These can be either individual sessions, or sessions that are part of a sequence of work which you have undertaken.

34

Performance Criteria

The performance criteria for Unit B22 are aimed at collecting evidence that will demonstrate your competence to plan training and teaching sessions. They also provide evidence of your personal confidence and your professional competence.

You must collect evidence to show you have considered the overall purposes of the sessions you have presented, as well as the practicalities of the planning decisions you have taken.

You must indicate that you have taken into account both locational and organisational considerations when planning your teaching sessions. These include the nature of the room in which you teach, its size and how it is set out, as well as the range of available resources and the learning needs of your students.

Your evidence should include:

- the aims and objectives you have selected for the individual sessions

- the intellectual level of the work you will undertake with the group

- the pace of presentation learners can cope with

- the duration and overall structure of the teaching sessions

- the work done in past sessions and the purpose and content of future ones

- the range of possible ways in which sessions might be delivered

- the type of activities and learning experiences you have selected for your group

- the resources available and their suitability for the teaching methods you have selected. You should take into account such factors as age, appropriateness, the objectives of the session, the promotion of equal opportunities and access, special needs, ease of use and access, the overall organisation of the session and its fitness for purpose

35

Knowledge Evidence

The knowledge evidence for Unit B22 requires you to show your understanding of the following:

- why your teaching sessions need to be planned in a logical, sequenced and systematic way

- how you tackled this, taking into account the age, ability, aptitude and attitude of your students.

In particular your portfolio should indicate your knowledge and understanding of the following:

- the difference between aims and objectives, and how you made them appropriate and achievable as well as sequential

- the need for each teaching session to meet both your overall aims and the session objectives

- the importance of the effect of group size on possible teaching approaches and management strategies

- the ways in which adults learn most successfully and their individual learning preferences

- how learners are to meet the objectives of the session using the activities you have selected, and how this may impact on different learners within your group

- the implications of using different resources and the need to use a variety of resources to break up long teaching sessions, and to ensure the availability of equipment in good working order

- the methods you will use to evaluate the effectiveness of sessions you have delivered

- the ways to promote equality of opportunity and non-discriminatory practice

- The different approaches available towards designing successful teaching materials

- the implications for your sessions and the learning of others of the choice of strategies you make

36

B33: Prepare and develop resources to support learners

This unit relates to the preparation of teaching resources for your presentations. B331 focuses on the preparation of materials and facilities to support learning, while B332 concentrates on developing appropriate classroom resources.

Performance Criteria

The performance criteria for this unit relate to the production of effective resources. This effectiveness can often be best observed in a practical teaching situation. There are strong links between this unit and many of the requirements of the C units, described in the next chapter. To complete this unit successfully, you must show that the resources you have used are appropriate to meet the needs of your learners.

Resources are aids used to enhance the presentation of your teaching material and include hardware as well as software. Hardware resources include overhead projectors (OHPs) flipcharts, tape recorders and VCRs while software resources include photographs, diagrams and paper-based materials such as lecture notes or handouts.

The standards for this unit state that the resources used must meet three criteria. These are:

- their suitability for the purpose for which you use them

- their relationship to the objectives of the session

- their appropriateness for the room where the learning is taking place.

Your evidence for this unit must show that these resources are realistic, suitable for your learners and cost effective, and should demonstrate the care you have taken when producing them. This might include the need for written resources (such as handouts and OHPs):

37

- to be without grammatical and spelling errors,

- to be in a print or font style suitable for the size and ability level of the group

- to be produced within any budgetary constraints that may be imposed to meet the requirements of the Copyright Licensing Agency (CLA)

Where problems have occurred with the practical use of resources, such as inappropriateness of the materials or organisational problems within your classroom, your evidence must also indicate how you identified difficulties, reflected on them and made changes where this was appropriate.

Where appropriate, you should outline how your resources are available to your learners for their own use. You should also indicate in your evidence how they can be stored successfully for further use.

Knowledge Evidence

The knowledge evidence for B33 relates to your understanding of the range of resources available for you to use to aid your teaching. Written materials include handouts and notes for your learners, while visual materials include overhead transparencies (OHTs) which have been produced for you or those you have made yourself as well as audio or video material you may have used. It is important that your portfolio of evidence shows how you have selected appropriate resources for particular learners.

Your portfolio should also indicate how you have prepared and used written and visual material to promote learning or have adapted materials to suit your learners better. The adaptations may include changing something to make a concept or its language clearer for a learner with reading difficulties, or altering learning material in some way: for example you may have enlarged the print on a handout to make it more accessible to someone with visual difficulties.

38

Your portfolio should also provide evidence of your knowledge of the principles of presenting resources and prepared materials to learners, and the potential problems of using inappropriate materials. Here you may need to consider:

- The vocabulary of your learners

- The way you have structured the material – is it up to date, logical and sequenced appropriately? Does it meet your objectives? Is it professionally produced and attractive to the learners?

- The medical condition of your learners – have any of them eyesight or hearing problems which may cause them difficulties with the resources you have produced? Do they have disabilities that make concentration difficult? How can you adjust your resources to meet their needs?

Your evidence must also show your awareness of the problems associated with the use of discriminatory language (for example, racist or sexist language) and how you have overcome these difficulties in the resources you have produced. Similarly the evidence you are presenting should demonstrate your awareness of equal opportunities legislation and followed good practice associated with it when preparing or choosing resources. Good practice might include having a gender balance in the examples you present to your learners or including examples suitable for an ethnic mix of people.

Your portfolio must also show you have taken into account health and safety factors when using and storing your resources, as set out in the Health and Safety at Work Act (1974). This Act provides a framework of regulations intended to prevent people coming to harm at work. As a teacher you have a duty to see that your learners come to no harm. In relation to your evidence for this unit, you must show that you understand the importance:

- having a well lit, warm and appropriately ventilated teaching room

- following correct operating procedures and manufacturer's instructions when using resources,

- being safety conscious, especially where there are trailing wires or extension leads from electrical resources

- making use of technical support to provide information about the safe use of electrical or mechanical resources

- knowing the health and safety legislation which applies to the use and storage of resources

39

UNDERPINNING KNOWLEDGE

Included here are some of the areas of background knowledge you may need when preparing lessons and planning resources.

Lesson Preparation

Your portfolio should provide evidence of your knowledge that successful lessons are based on the successful management of people, materials and resources. It is arguable that the art of successful classroom management lies in preparation and the thought given to it.

You should also demonstrate that your lesson planning has two functions, to provide a strategy for your teaching and to give a series of cues for your learners to be used during the session. Your lesson plans are intended to help you move logically through a series of points during a lesson, covering essential information based around predetermined objectives. Your lesson plan should be flexible, and should also show that you will accommodate contributions made by the group members.

Initial Planning

Initial planning relates both to the resources you are considering using and to the overall organisation of the session. You need to show in your evidence that you have thought about how you have sequenced the various key points of your session to make it both manageable for yourself and coherent for your learners. It is also important at this stage that you consider the strategies which you will use at the beginning and end of the session and the resources that will most effectively help you put over your points.

To complete your evidence on initial planning successfully you need to consider the following points:

- What point in the teaching programme have you reached? Have your learners understood and how much have they learned? (Indeed, what are your criteria for learning success?)

- What do you need to teach next

- How will you do this? (This latter point should include your indication of the expected learning in the session, approaches to the differentiation of learning materials and strategies to be used.)

Aims and objectives

The evidence in your portfolio needs to show that you are clear about the breakdown of the skills, knowledge and understanding to be achieved by your learners in each session that you lead. It will also need to show how you have taken account of the pace at which your learners can learn and the appropriate level of information for them. It is from these considerations that the aims and objectives of your sessions can be made. You need to show that you have an understanding of the importance of setting aims and objectives for your lessons.

The **aim** of a session is its overall purpose and what you expect the learner or learners will have achieved by the time it is completed.

The **objectives** of a session are the aims broken down into achievable smaller parts. Sometimes these achievable parts are called targets, and they can be individual to each learner, taking into account such factors as the point their learning has achieved, and the pace of their learning. Objectives often indicate the sequence of the teaching that is being given. Objectives should be precise (often they are set round actions). Where possible, objectives should be measurable. This measuring (usually described as testing or assessment) can take a number of different forms. These are discussed in greater detail in Chapter 6.

41

Accommodation

Your portfolio needs information about the accommodation you use for teaching. If there are variations in this accommodation then the effects of this on your delivery or on the availability of resources might also be discussed. Within your portfolio you need to show that you have where necessary considered the following points:

- the organisation of classroom displays

- booking a suitable location

- hiring or borrowing a video

- making sure that reprographics are on time

- booking a speaker

- preparing a collection of resources to support independent learning

Lesson plans

Your portfolio should provide outlines of two of your planned sessions. Lesson plans can take a variety of formats, one of which is shown as fig. 7 below.

Your formal lesson plans should contain the following information:

- the title of the lesson
- details of the class

A Session Plan

Group:

Date: Time:

Introducing the session

The introduction should cover such aspects as

- work already covered
- aims and objectives of the lesson
- question/answer session

Developing the session

This stage should indicate the main components of the session content, and should be closely linked to the stated objectives of the session. This part of the plan should provide details of the instruction, experiences, learning and reflection that are to take place.

Concluding the session

This part of the session should take into account any assessment (either formal or informal) conducted as a result of the teaching that has been undertaken. It should include indications of the approaches you will use to draw together the main points of your session and also, where appropriate, some pointers to the content of your next session.

Fig 7: An outline plan for a typical session

- the time of the lesson
- details of prior learning
- the objective(s) of the lesson

Some idea of the timing of events may be usefully provided in a lesson plan. You should show how any timescale you provide is only an estimate and it may not be appropriate to stick to it rigidly in practice. There are a number of reasons for this, usually concerned with the need to be flexible. This allows you to use part of the lesson for dealing with some other issue which has arisen or for allowing learner participation to be fully explored.

Approaches to Teaching

It is important that the teaching strategies you use in the sessions included in your portfolio are selected with care in order to 'put over' the information in a clear, interesting and succinct way. It is also important that you show that you are able to respond flexibly to classroom situations.

You will also need to consider the possibility of differentiating material for your learners. This may involve the simplification of material for those with learning difficulties or changing its normal appearance for those with particular disabilities or the extension of tasks for your more able learners. Examples might include enlarging text or altering the seating arrangements for someone who has sight difficulties, or changing the colour of the paper for those with specific learning difficulties.

Presentations

Your portfolio should show your awareness of the variety of ways in which a presentation may be made. Some commonly used approaches are listed below. The approaches listed are not mutually exclusive and they are sometimes known by other names.

- brainstorming
- brains trusts
- case studies
- coaching

43

- debates
- demonstrations
- discovery methods
- field trips
- independent learning
- interviews
- laboratory work
- projects
- questionnaires
- role-play
- seminars
- team teaching
- tutorials
- work cards
- workshops.

44 Teaching aids

There is a range of aids available to assist your teaching. These include blackboards, whiteboards and magnetic boards, projectors (overhead, film and slide), recorders (cassette and video), audio and audio-visual equipment (radio, TV, stereo), and visual aids (handouts, worksheets, charts, posters, books and magazines). You need to show what factors you have taken into account when selecting your teaching aids. You should show that you have thought about:

- What information is to be provided?
- How is this best done?
- What is the most effective way?
- How is learning efficiency best achieved?
- With which aids do we feel most comfortable?

Your portfolio should also indicate an awareness of the purpose and impact of the visual aids you have selected. You might consider whether you want to:

- Provide concrete/quasi-concrete experiences. (Videos and some IT aids are particularly valuable here)

- Develop motivation and interest

- Increase retention of information. (To have seen pictures of something or heard about it is a good secondary experience that can only be bettered by actually taking part or being there)

- Provide a variety of approaches to learning

- Ensure there is a focus to the lesson, thus providing the best use of class contact time. Develop communications with yourself and the learner. Learners can take in information from an OHT at their own pace (leave it long enough for them to do so) or assimilate information from a video or audiotape

- Ensure that work based on individual needs. Different learners can be set different tasks if this is felt to be appropriate, or their individual needs can be met by differentiating the material.

45

Recording work completed

Your portfolio needs to show that you have kept a record of the work you have done with a class. Recording work can be very helpful for your lesson planning. A record of work completed successfully will enable you to review student progress as well as providing you with a reminder not only of what you have taught, but also of the sequence of steps you used. Recording work completed will also help you with your lesson evaluation. More can be read about how to approach this in Chapter 7. Remember you need to present two lesson plans as part of your portfolio.

Other considerations

For the successful completion of the B units your portfolio should also include evidence that you have considered the following important questions

- How have you ensured that you have the full participation of students in your lesson and that you have provided leadership to facilitate their learning effectively?

- How you have adjusted your language style so that it is appropriate for the class? In this context it is important to show how you have developed channels of communication with your students. It is also important that you are aware of the importance of non-verbal communication skills in your teaching?

Your portfolio should also show that you have critically assessed and reflected on what you have done, and why the session went well or badly. Questions you may ask include what were the good and bad points of the session, and did you cover the teaching material you expected? You might indicate what you would change next time and how you would go about changing it.

You also need to think about the size of your audience. In some circumstances particular forms of presentation will be inappropriate, and if this has been a consideration you should make clear the decisions you made and why you made them. Other factors you need to show you have considered include:

- the size of the room in which you are making your presentation

46

- the age of the audience. Some older learners have greater difficulties with certain forms of presentation, as have those who have never experienced a particular method before

- the composition of your audience

- their learning expectations.

CASE STUDIES

Here are a number of case studies of candidates who have successfully presented evidence of competence for the units described in this chapter. To help you, these case studies are drawn from a variety of teaching and training sources.

Unit B22

Case study 1

Brian is a lecturer in further education and provided evidence of how he prepared sessions for young adults undertaking NVQ Level 1 in Administration. The evidence which follows is taken from work he did with units for the qualification on stock control, and required two sessions.

- a diagram matching learning options to learning needs

- Details of the learning options he selected to meet the group's needs, accompanied by his rationale for choice and a list of the factors he considered

- a plan of the room layout, indicating equipment available

- a list of resources and people who will provide support, including the materials, equipment and other facilities he needed to deliver the sessions

- a session plan outlining aims and objectives, activities, timings, resources and the evaluation methods used to test the group's understanding

- a further session plan adapted for an individual learner, explaining how objectives will be met

- an explanation of how he planned to deal with issues of equal opportunities and non-discrimination, including disability, age, ethnic origin, culture, religion, gender, and sexual orientation

Case Study 2

Margaret is a trainer employed by a training company to deliver a customised Health and Safety course to employees of a client company. Her evidence included:

- a training needs analysis detailing the company's training requirements

- a list of the topics to be covered and the durations of the sessions

- details of training options chosen to meet individual needs explaining factors which could affect delivery

- a list of resources including details of technical support, materials, equipment and facilities available

- two session plans, one for a small group and one for an individual

- a copy of an evaluation questionnaire used at the end of the session to check understanding

- an explanation of how the training company promotes equal opportunities and non-discriminatory practice with clients

Case study 3

Elaine is a special needs assistant in a comprehensive school working with twelve and thirteen year old children with reading difficulties. Her evidence:

- a statement outlining the learning needs of individuals and the support she was required to provide

48

- a statement identifying the topics to be covered in the session

- a list of activities she has identified as being appropriate to the needs of the children, accompanied by a rationale for her choice

- a list of resources required, including details of students in the sixth form who assisted with the reading exercises and lists of books, equipment and facilities

- one session plan designed for a group of three children and another designed for an individual, including the aims, objectives, facilities available, group activities selected, resources used and methods of recording progress

- a testimonial from the school's special needs co-ordinator who confirmed her competence to support children effectively

- a rationale explaining how she promoted equal opportunities and non-discriminatory practice and identifying relevant factors that could affect delivery

Unit B33

Case study 1

Julie is a basic skills tutor in the Learning Support Centre of a further education college teaching a lesson on spelling to adults. For this unit her evidence comprised:

- references to lesson plans

- notes on choice of resources, including costs, availability and suitability for meeting learners' needs

- an example of adapting learning aids: she produced a crossword game from a worksheet, which proved to be an interesting and enjoyable way for her learners to improve their spelling

- a 'Countdown' spelling quiz, based on the television programme: she developed this quiz to help learners identify vowels and consonants

- examples of overhead projector transparencies used to explain spelling rules

- a report on an assessed session

- a bibliography, available to her as a Teacher's Aid

- a student evaluation questionnaire to determine preference for different learning aids

- an annotated health and safety policy statement, indicating the key points affecting her work in the centre

- an annotated equal opportunities policy statement outlining the key issues

- a statement that confirms her understanding of copyright regulations, with accompanying leaflets

- a statement outlining the accessibility and storage of materials in the Learning Support Centre

- annotated reference material on the use of different classroom resources

49

Case study 2

Jim is a trainer in the Prison Service who is involved in staff development training and delivering courses to prisoners. Confidentiality of information is a major consideration when presenting evidence from this environment. His evidence included:

- references to session plans

- a summary of training courses he has delivered and a profile of the different learners

- a plan of the training room layout with equipment available

- notes relating to role-play scenarios and simulated activities used during his training sessions

- a statement from his assessor confirming the examination of overhead projector transparencies, handouts and printout from an electronic flipchart: these contained confidential information and therefore could not be included in his portfolio

- a statement outlining his understanding and implementation of equal opportunities policy, non-discriminatory practice, health and safety regulations and copyright law

- evaluation questionnaires completed by anonymous learners

- a comparison between the two training groups and how he needed to adapt materials to meet their differing needs. He identified restrictions he encountered on the content of handouts

- a confirmation of questioning by the assessor about the storage of materials.

50

REFERENCE TO OTHER UNITS

The evidence you have collected for the units described in this chapter may be cross-referenced to evidence for the B units as well as the following Level 3 elements in other units:

- A222 'Identify learning needs with individuals'
- B222 'Design training and development sessions for learners'
- C221 'Negotiate learning programmes with learners'
- C272 'Facilitate collaborative learning'
- C232 'Facilitate exercises and activities to promote learning in groups'
- E211 'Select methods for evaluating training and development programmes'
- E212 'Collect information to evaluate training and development programmes'

as well as units

- C21 'Create a climate conducive to learning'
- C24 'Facilitate learning through demonstration and instruction'
- D11 'Monitor and review progress with learners'

SUMMARY

This chapter described the performance evidence required for your portfolio for the City and Guild Level 3 B units. These units are concerned with designing learning programmes for your learners and the resources that are an integral part of their presentation.

The underpinning knowledge for these units covers your preparation and planning, identifying aims and objectives in your teaching, the presentation of your teaching sessions, the recording of work completed and the need to think about the availability of appropriate resources.

CHAPTER FIVE

The C Units
Practical Classroom
Management

Introduction

The City and Guilds C units focus on the practicalities of teaching and training and the situation and conditions in which teaching takes place. In these units particular stress is placed on:

- the relationship between learning theories and the practicalities of classroom presentation and management for both individual learners and groups

- the selection of appropriate teaching methods

- the range of information and communication technology (ICT) available to support you and your learners,

- resource constraints influencing the selection and use of approaches to learning and teaching

- strategies for evaluating teaching and resources in terms of their efficiency and effectiveness.

For these units, materials to demonstrate your competence can best be obtained through the collection of 'active' evidence of your observed practice in the classroom.

At NVQ Level 3 there are six units. These are C21: Create a climate conducive to learning, C23: Facilitate learning in groups through presentation and activities, C22: Agree learning programmes with learners, C24: Facilitate learning through demonstration and instruction, C25: Facilitate leaning through coaching and C27: Facilitate group learning.

Units C21 and C23, which can often be undertaken together, are directed towards the presentation of lessons to your learners and your classroom management and organisational skills. Unit C21 is concerned with how you create a positive learning climate, while unit C23 is aimed at collecting evidence about your skills at enabling learning to take place as a result of the presentations you have made and the learning activities you have set your learners. The other C units relate to particular aspects of classroom management. These include demonstrating your competence when negotiating learning programmes with your learners (C22), facilitating learning through classroom demonstration and instruction (C24), the use of coaching techniques (C25) and facilitating learning in groups (C27).

PORTFOLIO REQUIREMENTS

54 **C21: Create a climate conducive to learning**

Unit C21 has four elements. C211 is concerned with establishing a rapport, C212 with supporting learners' needs, C213 with promoting access to learning and C224 with promoting anti-discriminatory practice.

This unit is concerned with the practicalities of your personal organisation and management within the classroom. Performance evidence is best collected in realistic situations. Suitable examples might include observation reports from your tutor or your peers, or by witness statements collected from your learners.

Performance Criteria

The first part of the evidence needed for unit C21 is concerned with setting a positive working environment for your learners. The performance requirements focus on evidence you can produce to demonstrate that you can successfully meet the individual needs of your learners, and your professional skills in providing quality time for them.

Your portfolio of evidence should indicate clearly your practical skills in listening to your learners and making them feel relaxed and able to participate fully in your sessions. Your evidence could show this through demonstrating your classroom skills when listening to them:

- participating in group discussions

- answering questions

- making comments

- indicating their personal learning concerns

Beyond this, your evidence should also demonstrate your skills in:

- handling the individual views and beliefs of members of your groups in a non-judgmental fashion

- being aware of verbal and non-verbal forms of communication and the effects of body language in classroom situations

- dealing in a sensitive manner with difficulties that might occur

55

This unit also concentrates on presenting of evidence that shows how you have promoted access to learning and assessed your learners. This part of your evidence should indicate, in practical terms, how you eliminate any of the barriers that might prevent from learners from maximising their learning potential. Such barriers include:

- physical factors, such as access to the classroom or to equipment

- psychological factors, such as learners' attitude to learning or to other members of the group

- emotional factors, such as their ability to cope under pressure

- social factors

- ineffective methods of delivery

- unsuitable materials, ideas and concepts

Your evidence should also show that you have an even-handed approach to your students and how you have avoided personal prejudices when working with them. Observation of your performance, by your tutors or other colleagues should show that you avoid personal bias when dealing with:

- age

- social background

- gender

- race

- sexual orientation

- physical appearance

- learning disability

To demonstrate your practical skills in promoting access to learning and achievement for your students, your portfolio should show how you provide advice and information for them about other available services. You should be aware of:

56

- learners' rights to accurate information about programmes and qualifications available to them, so you can match these to their needs and aspirations

- the previous learning experiences of your learners, so you can produce a coherent programme for them to match their current and future needs.

In presenting evidence of your skills in supporting your learners' needs, you will need to show that you have a working knowledge of the relevant legislation on equal opportunities and anti-discriminatory practice and the relevant documentation produced by your organisation. Evidence to show your practical skills in this area can come through your observed classroom practice, and should demonstrate your skills at dealing with the rights of individual learners and ensuring that these are upheld and promoted in accordance with current legislation and workplace policies.

Your evidence showing your awareness of how additional support for learners can be obtained should demonstrate your ability to provide information about:

- sources of information about additional support to which they might be entitled to enhance their learning

- support available within their place of work or in the institution where they are being taught

- any other available sources of further information and guidance

- how to contact guidance services for students within your organisation, for example, the counselling service, the industrial chaplain or the special needs team

- which members of staff can be contacted to provide information about obtaining specialist outside help, for example, a 'signer' for someone who is deaf

- agencies or other professionals providing specialist outside help

- how to initiate the complaints procedure for your students

57

Your evidence should also show that when you have referred learners who need support, you have done this in a constructive and supportive manner.

If you have not dealt with a live situation in which these issues have arisen, you should provide information about what you would do in such circumstances. This information may be part of your knowledge evidence for this unit.

Your performance evidence for this unit must also demonstrate that you do not exploit your relationship with learners, or abuse your role. You must show that you can identify and deal appropriately with discriminatory behaviour from others in the group. In this situation, 'appropriately' may mean demonstrating either how you have successfully dealt with such situations personally, or your knowledge of disciplinary procedures and where you can obtain information. In circumstances where a complaint was made and such procedures invoked, you must provide evidence of your positive support for learners.

You must also take into account both national legislation and organisational policy on anti-discriminatory practice. Examples of this are where the behaviour or language of others caused problems for an individual or group in your class, or where bullying was reported.

If you have had to deal with such a situation, you will need to show what action was taken and how the anti-discriminatory behaviour was dealt with. You might include:

- observations showing that your personal practice is not only of a high standard but is also consistent with both national legislation and organisational practice

- witness statements outlining a naturally occurring problem, details of your response to it and the support that you gave to the complainant.

58 Again, where you have not yourself had to deal with such a situation, your evidence will need to indicate what you would do and to whom you would turn for guidance in such circumstances.

As with the promotion of access to learning, your evidence must indicate where appropriate guidance on anti-discriminatory practice can be obtained from within your place of work.

Knowledge evidence

The knowledge requirements for C21 are related to theories of classroom management and practice. Some of them are similar to those for the B units. The requirements include the establishment of a good classroom atmosphere, making participants feels comfortable, as well as the interpretation both verbal and non-verbal communications.

You should have a working knowledge of current anti-discriminatory literature and equal opportunities legislation. You should also be aware of ways of promoting the rights of individuals with whom you work. Bearing in mind your evidence for unit A22, your knowledge of possible further training routes for your learners would be useful here as well. You should also be aware of your institution's Health and Safety regulations and the referral procedure adopted.

C22: Agree learning programmes with learners

This unit focuses on the decisions that you have made in conjunction with your learner, when first negotiating and then reviewing their learning programme. Element C221 concentrates on the negotiation process, while C222 focuses on the review of the programme. As with the other C units the evidence for C22 must be drawn from 'live' teaching experiences, as simulations are not acceptable as evidence. The evidence relating to the negotiation with learners must be drawn from your experience of negotiating with different types of learners and learning programmes. It should also show your skills in working both with individual learners and with groups.

Performance Criteria

The evidence to meet the performance criteria for unit C22 must show how you have deployed your skills when negotiating a programme of work with learners. You must show that:

- You made an accurate assessment of learners' individual needs, capabilities and personal aspirations

- You clearly explained the constraints on their learning opportunities

- You clearly explained the teaching methodology used and the ways of working

- You clearly explained the resources available

- You clearly explained progression routes towards further learning opportunities and qualifications

- You gave learners sufficient information and advice for them to make valid decisions about their requirements

- You encouraged learners to feel comfortable and to express their desires and concerns as well as to ask questions about the programme offered

- Where there were difficulties they were recognised, thought through and resolved in a way that maintained the working relationship between yourself and your learners

This unit also concentrates on reviewing the agreed programme with your learners. To meet the performance requirements your portfolio must also provide evidence of your skills in the following areas:

- When the programme of learning was reviewed, this information was shared and agreed with the learners.

- The methods used in the review and its time-scale were negotiated.

- Learners felt comfortable about contributing to the review.

- The learning programme could be justified by you and your learners to others who may be interested.

- Results of the review were recorded and passed on to others for use in an agreed manner.

- Any appropriate changes in the learning programme as a consequence of the review were agreed with learners and others involved.

Knowledge evidence

The knowledge evidence for this unit is concerned with classroom management issues and the positive management of your learners. Your portfolio should show your knowledge of the following:

- ways of putting learners at ease

- methods of delivering programmes for learners based on their needs, their learning styles, their preferences, their aspirations, the requirements of their role and the opportunities that are available for them

- useful strategies for finding out your learners' views about their personal learning aspirations

- the effect of group size and composition on the presentation of a learning programme

- the resources available to teach the programme

- how to promote, introduce and negotiate a programme of learning

- how to sequence and pace information, and select appropriate vocabulary, when presenting a programme of work

- progression and qualification routes for your learners

- equal opportunities legislation, anti-discriminatory practice and health and safety legislation as they affect the place where you do your teaching

C23: Facilitate learning in groups, through presentation and activities

This unit has two elements: C231, which relates giving presentations to groups of learners, and C232, which concentrates on facilitating learning with a group of learners using exercises and activities. Essentially this unit focuses on your ability to demonstrate sound class control while working with groups of learners.

61

Performance Criteria

The performance criteria for this unit are concerned with the quality of presentations you make to your learners. You must take into account the size of the group you are working with as well as its composition. Group size is defined in the awarding body's standards: small groups are those having fewer than six participants; large groups, those with more than twelve. The composition of a group relates to the level of skill and knowledge of the learners as well as their previous understanding of the work you are doing.

The standards for C23, like those for C21, state that learners must be comfortable with work presented to them. The teaching points you wish to make must be accessible to your learners. You should ensure that you have made clearly the points you wish to make and be able to ask questions and discuss issues they are concerned about, in a positive and professionally supportive atmosphere.

You should also demonstrate clearly in your evidence that you are able to pitch the content of your sessions at an appropriate level for the needs of all in your group, and that you can provide legible visual aids and resources to support the teaching in which you are engaged. You must show too that you can make adjustments where necessary.

The performance requirements also include managing groups of learners using the rules, norms and expectations you set for your teaching area. The members of the group should be clearly aware of the classroom activities you are setting for them and how these should be performed. This can be shown most easily through the clarity of your instructions and the level of presentation of the session.

Knowledge Evidence

For unit C23 the knowledge requirements relate to theories of classroom practice and management. They are diverse, and many of them can be related to those required for the B units. They include:

- ways of adapting classroom materials

- approaches for structuring classroom activities and making successful presentations

- approaches for putting learners at their ease

- techniques for sequencing and pacing sessions correctly

- questioning techniques for eliciting information from learners and for making them feel they are able to participate fully in your sessions

- the provision of constructive feedback

- an understanding of equal opportunities and anti-discriminatory practice.

C24: Facilitate learning through demonstration and instruction

Unit C24 focuses on the skills of demonstration and instruction as a teaching technique. The unit is concerned with the planning that must be done before a demonstration is given and the use of questioning and supervised practice.

To meet the requirements for this unit you must provide evidence that you have worked with groups of different sizes using different techniques. These techniques will depend on the size of the group and the approach being used.

You should also provide evidence that you have used at least two different activities with learners. One of these sessions should have been observed. As with the rest of the C units, simulations are not appropriate and your evidence must be drawn from real teaching situations.

Performance Criteria

The performance criteria for unit C24 focus on producing evidence of your techniques when demonstrating and instructing skills and methods to learners. They should show that:

- the learning programme takes into account an accurate analysis of the component techniques to be taught and the sequence in which this should be done

- the instruction is based on clearly identified learning objectives

- the demonstrations reflect real practice as closely as possible and are paced and sequenced to maximise learning

- the equipment used to make the demonstrations is realistic and, if there are significant differences, these should be pointed out to the learners.

- your learners are encouraged to ask questions and make comments at appropriate stages in the demonstration

- factors preventing efficient learning are identified and explored with individuals

63

- learners are encouraged to practise the skills that have been demonstrated and given further demonstrations if appropriate

- where instructions have been given, the learners' understanding is checked regularly and the instructions are modified

- positive, encouraging feedback is given to learners if necessary to help them to achieve the programme objectives.

- the demonstrations are set up in a way that allows for maximum visibility for those watching, while conforming to health and safety regulations; distractions and interruptions are kept to a minimum

- clear, accurate and appropriate summary information is provided to reinforce key points

Knowledge evidence

The knowledge evidence to fulfil the requirements of this unit should show that you have an understanding of:

- presenting demonstrations and giving instructions to learners

- factors that can inhibit learning

- the choice of appropriate equipment

- the need to take into account health and safety regulations

C25: Facilitate learning through coaching

Unit C25 has two elements: C251, which is concerned with coaching individual learners and C252, which is about assisting individuals to apply their learning. The purpose of the unit is to demonstrate that you are able to plan, develop and evaluate coaching sessions. Your performance evidence for this unit must cover at least two coaching sessions.

The definition of coaching provided in the City and Guilds candidate pack confines it to work with individual learners. However, coaching can be part of normal classroom practice when a number of learners are present but individual tasks are set for them. Coaching implies learning that has a strong practical focus.

Performance criteria

To meet the performance criteria for unit C25 you must demonstrate that you are competent to identify, plan and execute successfully a variety of coaching tasks. You should consider including evidence of how you went about:

- informally assessing the needs of your learners

- successfully identifying individual learning style to make teaching them effective

- setting appropriate and realistic objectives

- analysing the skills you wish to teach

- breaking down the skills to be taught into an appropriate and logical sequence

- Identifying manageable chunks of learning so that your learner will be presented with practical, clearly structured tasks

- conducting the session at an appropriate level and pace and providing learners with opportunities for practising their skills and applying what they have learned

- checking the progress of your learners in order to make adjustments to your teaching

- Providing positive and encouraging feedback to your learners to help them achieve their learning objectives

- checking on factors which might affect the learning efficiency of your learners,

- providing them with information about other people and resources available to help them with their learning

Knowledge evidence

Your knowledge evidence for C25 is concerned firstly with your knowledge of the wide range of available opportunities for learners and secondly with your understanding of negotiating with learners in a way that takes their preferred learning style into account. You must show your understanding of those factors which may inhibit learning, particularly where students:

- lack experience of formal learning,

- are apprehensive about learning

- compare themselves and their abilities and skills unfavourably with other learners.

You should also provide evidence of your knowledge of the following:

- putting learners at their ease and making them feel comfortable in a one-to-one situation

- negotiating learning objectives with your students

- breaking learning into small, manageable sections with clear objectives, so that you are coaching at the correct level of instruction and pace of delivery

- factors that inhibit learning in students and appropriate strategies for alleviating this

- developing your skills when instructing learners through the use of activities. For example, you should show your understanding of how to:

  - working to objectives and targets

  - sequencing activities appropriately for your students

  - dividing the task being taught into appropriate small steps

  - integrating theory and practice in the material being taught

- organising flexible coaching sessions so that you can make use of learning opportunities arising out of the work you and your learners are doing

- strategies for checking on learners' progress

- informal assessment both during and after your coaching sessions

66

- including incompatibility of learning styles, student anxiety, incorrect level or pace of instruction, misunderstanding of the tasks to be done and setting inappropriate targets

C27: Facilitate group learning

Unit C27 focuses on your understanding of how learners in groups interact and how you manage the resulting complex web of relationships which develop. You should demonstrate your understanding of the importance of group dynamics not only among learners but also between them and yourself, and your practical skills at dealing with this so that effective learning can take place. Your evidence should show how you have organised your teaching sessions to promote collaborative learning and avoid disruptive and challenging behaviour and also how you have helped individuals to reflect on their roles within the group.

Performance Criteria

To meet the performance criteria for unit C27 your evidence must demonstrate your practical skills in ensuring that:

the successful management of learning was negotiated in the **67** light of the tasks to be accomplished, taking into account the dynamics of the group

- the progress your learners made was properly monitored, and appropriate feedback was given in a positive and encouraging manner

- factors that influence learning were explored with your group and power, authority and influence appropriately used

- if conflict occurred it was dealt with appropriately, allowing learning to continue

- your teaching was appropriate to the size of the group and the level of your learners, was given at a pace they could cope with

- no stereotyping of learners or discrimination against them occurred, either through your teaching or the influence of others in the group

- your teaching was appropriately adapted to improve learning

Knowledge Evidence

The knowledge evidence for unit C27 requires an understanding of:

- strategies for putting groups at ease

- different adult learning styles

- appropriate activities for encouraging learning

- resources available for helping your learners

- methods of sequencing information and of presenting it at an appropriate level and pace for your group

- methods of monitoring learners' progress in a group setting

- equal opportunities and anti-discriminatory legislation

UNDERPINNING KNOWLEDGE

The underpinning knowledge for the C units is concerned with the practicalities of classroom management and managing inter-personal relationships with your learners. These are crucial skills for anyone undertaking teaching and training. Positive inter-personal relationships are essential for classroom management. There is a wide range of issues involved in this. Your underpinning knowledge should include the following:

- managing teaching sessions

- questioning and 'active listening' skills

- non-verbal communication skills

- adhering to equal opportunities and anti-discriminatory and other relevant legislation

- working with groups

- supporting individual needs

- reducing aggressive behaviour

Managing sessions

Your evidence needs to show that you have knowledge of the possible ways of managing your teaching session and it should include the decisions that you have made. Cohen and Mannion (1983) detailed six approaches to managing lessons. These included the **teacher-centred lesson**, the **active learning** approach, the **lecture/discussion**, the **independent planning** session, the **group task-centred** approach and the **independent learning** approach.

Your portfolio must demonstrate that your approach was appropriate, and that you have taken into consideration factors such as the size of the room, the way it is set out, the resources available to you, your perceived outcomes and, most importantly, your learners. You should show your awareness of the various levels of ability of your learners, and your understanding that some may have a greater concentration span than others or be more easily motivated.

Establishing rapport/putting learners at ease

Your evidence should show that you are aware of strategies for making your learners feel welcome and comfortable with their learning and the learning environment. Without such feelings adults are more likely to vote with their feet and leave your sessions.

You may find it useful to link your knowledge evidence in this area of the C units with evidence you have collected for A22. You could successfully cross-reference between some of these units. For example, the evidence might include course publicity material and the literature about the course.

Asking questions/active listening

Your evidence should show your awareness of the importance of asking learners questions and actively listening to their answers. The quality of teaching and learning is essentially bound up with actively listening to learners and to the type and quality of questions asked. In human relationships a great deal of information is conveyed through non-verbal communication and body language.

Your knowledge evidence should indicate your awareness of these forms of communication.

Equal Opportunities legislation

In most cases, the establishment in which you do your teaching or training will have a policy that respects individuals and their rights. These policies are often derived from the national equal opportunities and anti-discriminatory legislation. Your evidence should indicate that you have a working knowledge of these, and that:

- all your learners' individual needs were met with your active support

- the needs of all those you work with were respected

- you provided a positive learning environment

- your learners' entitlement to access to learning was respected

- using active listening techniques with your learners

70
- the requirements of health and safety regulations were taken into account

- you considered the issues of bias and stereotyping in your relationships with your learners and in the resources you used

- you are aware of the agencies available to support your learners

It is important that your portfolio shows how you dealt in a non-judgmental way with:

- access for learners with disabilities: it is important to understand that this is not only a matter of access to the room but also of how learners are included in the activities going on there

- bias and stereotyping: this relates to your ability to work positively with everyone you teach regardless of any personal views you may hold about them. Essentially, you should show that you consider all your learners to be equal value

Health and Safety Legislation

The Health and Safety at Work Act (1974) and the Control of Substances Hazardous to Health (COSHH) regulations make it clear that teachers and trainers have a duty of care for their learners. As with the equal opportunities legislation, your portfolio must provide evidence of your working knowledge of this legislation.

Working in groups

Your evidence should show your awareness of the importance of **group dynamics** and the effect of this on the learning environment in your classes. This evidence might include ways in which you approached working with different groups of learners where there were clearly identifiable variations in the learning environment.

Support needs

You should show that you are aware that some learners may need extra help to complete the work or even to participate successfully in the classroom. You may also be able to show how you worked out a suitable solution with a learner. Examples you might consider include changing a learner's seating position or allowing extra time to complete work.

Some learners will need additional support with their learning. Many such needs arise as a result of medical, social or emotional factors rather than educational ones. Your knowledge evidence should show how these needs might be met and that you are aware of the following techniques:

- **adaptation** (enlarged print and audio-taping are examples of this)

- **differentiation** (for example, changing the vocabulary or the sentence structure to improve access)

- **physical support** within the classroom

- **specialist support** either internally or externally. (Examples might include help with dyslexia, individual counselling or social welfare services).

71

Your evidence should show not only who you might refer a learner to, but also who you might turn to for information and guidance. You may also need to indicate the names of people to contact, their location and the times they are available.

CASE STUDIES

Here are a number of case studies about learners who have successfully presented evidence of their competence for the units described in this chapter. To help you, these case studies have been drawn from a variety of teaching and training situations.

Unit C21
Case study 1

Anne is a lecturer in further education. She runs a course with a group of adult learners. Her evidence was gathered from the first four weeks of the course and included:

- details of icebreaker activities she has selected to develop group cohesion

- copies of a questionnaire completed by her group after the initial induction period

- a plan of the room layout identifying its good and bad points

- a list of the ground rules negotiated between herself and the group, identifying each other's expectations

- a copy of the student handbook issued to the group with annotated sections relating to

  - implementation of the equal opportunities policy

  - Learning Support Services available

  - the students' charter

  - the appeals procedure

  - how confidentiality of information is ensured and

  - implications of the Data Protection Act

  - the college's health and safety policy

- a rationale explaining how she establishes rapport with groups, refering to different body language signs and identifying constraints on communication

- a case study about how she provided support to a learner wishing to improve writing and research skills

- pre-course interview notes

- a rationale for the way she promotes equal opportunities and anti-discriminatory practice. Included in the rationale are accounts of specific incidents she has dealt with, confirming her knowledge of college procedures

- an assessment report of an observed teaching session

- records of the assessor questioning, confirming her knowledge and competence when supporting her trainers

Case study 2

Linda is a training co-ordinator delivering in-company training for the Retail National Vocational Course to recently recruited young adults. She used the following evidence to support her competence:

- information about icebreaker activities she uses

- details of role-play exercises, including objectives, with a videotape of group activities

- a room plan showing the seating arrangements and giving reasons for her choice of layout

- a list of agreed ground rules about behaviours, negotiated by the group

- examples of visual aids and handouts, with her justification for their use

- details of a field trip she arranged for the group, with the aims and objectives identified, including information about activities during the trip and her reasons for choosing them

- photographic evidence collected during the field trip

- an audio tape of a feedback session she conducted with the group on their return from the field trip

- an evaluation report of the field trip resulting from a discussion between herself and other trainers. This identified the group's achievements and suggested changes for future trips

- a rationale for the way she supports her groups referring to barriers

- an explanation of the way in which she promotes equal opportunities and anti-discriminatory practice in the training room

- an assessment report of an observed training session

- Testimonials from colleagues in the training department

Case study 3

Pam is Sugarcraft tutor to a group of mixed ability learners attending a community course in a village hall. This is a non-vocational ten-week course. The following evidence was included:

74

- a rationale for how she establishes rapport with learners and develops a social atmosphere to ensure they enjoy the weekly sessions

- an assessment report for observed teaching session

- a plan of the room layout with an accompanying statement identifying good and bad features of the facilities available

- leaflets providing course details

- a community education information leaflet

- details of informal interviews she conducted with learners before they joined the course

- an explanation of additional support she can offer learners, including finance, materials and disability aids

- an explanation of how she promotes equal opportunities with her group, including a policy document available to learners

- a copy of the community education disability statement

- an explanation of how she identifies barriers to learning and attempts to remove them

- health and safety information relating to her practice within the village hall

- a copy of the complaints procedure with an explanation of how it may be used

- a statement explaining her understanding of the Data Protection Act and confidentiality issues relating to her course

- a set of group exercises

Unit C23
Case study 1

Peter is a lecturer in further education delivering a General National Vocational Qualification (GNVQ) in Business Studies to young adults. He has responsibility for both intermediate and advanced groups. The intermediate group consists of 15 students and the advanced group of 6 students. The following evidence was collated for this unit:

75

- lesson plans explaining the aims and objectives of the sessions, with an accompanying rationale on his choice of teaching strategies

- a set of exercises he uses in the sessions, with an explanation of how they are designed to meet objectives

- copies of handouts containing supplementary information

- an assessment report of an observed teaching session

- details of activities he uses to develop group dynamics and integrate confident and unconfident students

- an explanation of how he controls groups, with reference to disciplinary incidents he has had to deal with

- a comparison of the different abilities and sizes of groups

- records of individual tutorial sessions where provision of student support was discussed and an action plan made

- reference material relating to equal opportunities and anti-discriminatory practice, with an explanation of how he has dealt with discriminatory behaviour and language

- an evidence log book recording his personal evaluation of selected sessions

Case study 2

Dorothy is a Basic Skills tutor teaching a group of adults of mixed ages and abilities. She included the following documentation for this unit:

- session plans identifying her aims and objectives

- an explanation of the group's initial behaviour and attributes, as well as topics she has selected to meet their learning needs

- copies of visual aids

- examples of exercises

- an assessment report of an observed teaching session

- a rationale explaining the composition of the group and of its members, including an explanation of the dynamics of the group

- an explanation of a method she uses to create group inter-action: this involves pairing higher and lower ability learners to offer support in reading and the completion of exercises

- a report on a verbal evaluation of a session by learners, and her written analysis of the feedback provided

Unit C24
Case study 1

Sandra, a nurse delivering training within a large hospital, demon-strates manual handling techniques to nursing and support staff caring for patients on the wards. Demonstrations are carried out in the hospital's training department, which is equipped to simulate the ward environment. Sandra also provides individual tuition in the community for support staff. Her evidence included:

- session plans for a group session and an individual session in lifting techniques for patients, which included a demonstration and instruction about procedures

- a list of equipment available for demonstrations in the training room. Sandra also specified the equipment she takes with her when training in the community

- a plan and photograph of the training room

- a prompt-list for demonstrations with critical points identified

- a report by her assessor on an observed demonstration and instruction session for a group of eight people

- a rationale for the way demonstrations are conducted, including methods of instruction used and factors to be considered

- examples of supplementary handouts referring to techniques used

Unit C25
Case study 1

Sue is a Special Needs assistant in a secondary school working with students who have been identified as requiring additional support. These students have regular reviews, and targets of achievement are set for each term. She completed this unit with the following evidence:

- two completed individual education plans; students' details were deleted to maintain confidentiality

- two lesson plans she designed for individuals

- a list of resources required to support and coach each individual, and her reasons for choosing them

- a copy of a handout she used, entitled 'Ways to help students remember'

- examples of lessons she has used, taken from reading books

- a play she used, which requires students to read aloud and interact with each other

- an assessment of an observed learning support session

- records of progress for each student, completed during and after sessions

- a rationale for how she plans her coaching, to facilitate learning and identify any barriers encountered

REFERENCE TO OTHER UNITS

Because of the nature of its practical relevance in classroom performance, evidence produced for the C units can be cross-referenced to a large number of other units. Evidence produced for unit C21, for example, can be cross-referenced to all the other Level 3 units. Other elements that are mentioned by the TDLB in this context:

- A222 'Identify learning needs with individuals'
- B221 'Identify options for training and development sessions'
- D324 'Make assessment decisions and provide feedback'
- B21 'Design learning programmes to meet learners' requirements'
- B33 'Prepare and develop resources to support learning'
- D11 'Monitor and review progress with learners'
- E31 'Evaluate and develop own practice'

78

SUMMARY

This chapter has concentrated on the collection of evidence for the six C units, which are concerned with practical classroom performance. These Units are about creating a positive learning environment for both individuals and for groups of learners.

Underpinning knowledge required for the C units relates to classroom management and the development of interpersonal skills. You must also show that you understand national equal opportunities and anti-discriminatory legislation, as well as health and safety policies.

CHAPTER SIX

The D Units Assessment

Introduction

The City and Guilds D units focus on the use of assessment methods to make assessment decisions and provide feedback to learners and candidates.

At NVQ Level 3 there are five units. D11: Monitor and review progress with learners and D21: Conduct non-competence based assessments are designed for assessors of learners who are not following a competence-based scheme such as an NVQ, but whose achievement has to be monitored and assessed to demonstrate progress towards objectives. D32: Assess candidate performance and D33: Assess candidate using differing sources of evidence and D36: Advise and support candidates to identify prior achievement are designed for assessors working with individuals who are taking NVQ awards.

PORTFOLIO REQUIREMENTS

D11: Monitor and review progress with learners

Unit D11 relates to evidence about your skills when formatively assessing learners, as a result of your teaching. This unit is about collecting information on the progress of your learners, providing them with structured feedback on this and appropriately modifying their plans for their future learning.

Unit D11 has three elements:

- Collecting information on learners' progress

- Conducting formative assessments with learners

- Reviewing progress with learners.

You will need to show in your evidence for this unit that you have conducted a formative assessment programme with at least two of your learners.

Performance Criteria

To satisfy the evidence requirements for this unit you need to demonstrate that:

- you explained to your learners the nature of formative assessment and the use to be made of any information you collect

- you have assessed your learners using the targets and learning objectives negotiated with them

- you gathered appropriate information about your learners to provide evidence of their performance, from a range of sources. (You are not however expected to use scientific research techniques),

- your methods of collecting this information were appropriate (valid and reliable) and met the requirements of the relevant awarding body

You should also show that you encouraged your learners to feel comfortable with the assessment process, and to ask questions and express their views. Your portfolio should also demonstrate that you took into account the pace and level at which learners can make progress and that you considered the requirements of the national legislation governing equal opportunities and anti-discriminatory practice.

To demonstrate your skills in interpreting assessment information, you must show how:

- your judgements can be justified

- you conducted assessments without bias

- you gave positive and encouraging feedback to your learners

- the information you collected from the assessments was collated, summarised and stored efficiently, and made available for others wishing to access it

- you used the information to effect changes in subsequent sessions

Knowledge Evidence

Your portfolio should show evidence of your knowledge of:

- the principles and purposes of formative assessment

- how to pace your instruction and appropriate language

- how to collect and analyse information about your learners' progress,

- what is meant by validity and reliability

- how to put learners at ease and provide them with the best environment for assessment

- how to give constructive feedback

- issues relating to equal opportunities legislation and anti-discriminatory practice

- how to summarise the information you have collected

- how to store sensitive information

- issues of confidentiality and the uses of information technology (IT) in record keeping

Suitable evidence for this unit may be drawn from a variety of sources, for example:

- an assessment record you used to review your learners' progress

- a timetable for meetings at which progress was discussed

- a chart showing the progress of a group of learners or a comparison of the progress of two learners

- an interim report produced by a third party who has an interest in your learner

Unit D21: Assess individuals for non-competence based assessment systems

Unit D21, like unit D11 above, relates to the assessment of non-competence based learning. However, this unit focuses largely on the collection of evidence for summative assessments (the assessment of progress towards stated objectives, often those set by external examination or awarding bodies).

Unit D21 has three elements:

- Conducting non-competence based assessments

- Analysing evidence to form an assessment decision

- Providing feedback to individuals on the assessment decision

Your evidence should show that you have worked on at least two non-competence assessments, analysed the subsequent results and provided feedback to your learners.

Performance Criteria

To meet the performance criteria for unit D21 you must demonstrate evidence of your skills at providing your learners or any other interested party with information on the requirements of assessment tasks. You should also provide evidence that your practice is up-to-date and meets the requirements set by the awarding body, and that, where relevant, approval has been obtained from the awarding body for you to act as an assessor. Further, your portfolio should demonstrate your awareness of factors that might impinge on your ability to manage the assessment process successfully.

You must also provide evidence of your ability to:

- carry out the assessment tasks successfully

- use the designated marking system correctly

- match performance to specified criteria

Your evidence should also show that:

- you have completed the tasks within the constraints of the resources available, and to an agreed time scale

- you have accurately recorded the results of the assessment in the specified documents

- any analysis of the results must have been undertaken fairly and without bias, and verified according to the assessment procedures

- the evidence you collected from the assessments is handled according to the rules of confidentiality

Finally, your portfolio must demonstrate your skills at providing feedback in a suitable atmosphere. Feedback should be constructive, positive and appropriate to the needs of your learners, and should show that you have encouraged them to discuss your decisions and their consequences, and to seek further advice.

Knowledge Evidence

83

Your evidence for unit D21 should demonstrate that you have knowledge of the principles, processes and methods of assessment, and of any factors that might encroach on them. This might include knowing about:

- how to administer tests, and the legal constraints placed on them or on those who administer them

- how to observe your learners

- the use of interview techniques and the different types of interview

- how to interpret and make decisions about evidence you have collected

- verification and assessment systems

- issues relating to equal opportunities and anti-discriminatory practice

- how to provide constructive feedback

- sources of useful advice available to you

Useful sources of evidence for unit D21 might include:

- schedules indicating the sequence of tasks to be assessed

- the time scale and any weighting of marks for the different tasks

- assessment instruments you have used, such as essays, assignments or practical tasks

- the regulations specified by the examination board or awarding body

- your feedback to learners justifying the grades you have given

- audio or video tapes of feedback sessions

- case study notes.

D32: Assess Candidate Performance

The NVQ model specifies a number of crucial requirements for the assessment and accreditation of evidence. These are described as the evidence requirements, and they are primarily concerned with the fairness of the assessment of candidates. They relate to the reliability, validity, authenticity and currency of the evidence presented.

Unit D32 is concerned with the process of collecting and judging evidence of a candidate's performance, against nationally agreed standards. These standards may apply to a whole award or to parts, such as individual units or elements.

Simulation is not acceptable to prove competence for this unit. You must assess a candidate's performance in a real working environment in the workplace, a training centre or at college.

The unit is divided into four elements:

- Agree and review a plan for assessing performance

- Collect and judge performance evidence against criteria

- Collect and judge knowledge evidence

- Make assessment decisions and provide feedback

The evidence presented must be derived from the assessment of a minimum of three areas of competence that have been agreed with a candidate. The evidence can be from different assessment opportunities. It is important that your evidence should be generated from naturally occurring situations and that the assessment opportunity is arranged with the full agreement of the candidate. It is important too that the assessment procedure is seen to be fair, realistic and accessible to all candidates, including those who have special assessment requirements.

Performance Criteria

The performance criteria for Unit D32 relates to:

- agreeing and reviewing a plan to assess a candidate's competence in at least three elements

- judging a candidate's natural performance in the three elements

- collecting and assessing knowledge through the observation of performance and the use of oral or written questions

- making assessment decisions and providing constructive feedback to candidates

Your evidence of agreeing and reviewing a plan to assess a candidate's performance should include:

- the name of the qualification to be assessed

- the title of the unit and elements to be assessed

- the assessment methods to be used (eg. natural performance, questioning, simulations)

- the evidence to be collected

- the location, time and date of the assessment

- any special facilities needed,

- a date for reviewing the plan

85

- details of others who should be consulted

- assessor and candidate signatures with dates, to confirm the plan was agreed

- how disagreements or problems during the planning process are to be dealt with

When planning for assessment it is important that the assessor understands the requirements of the elements to be assessed. The assessor needs to have experience of the subject area to be able to advise the candidate on methods of achievement evidence collection and resolve any problems that may arise. Since unit D32 relates to the assessment of both performance and knowledge, opportunities for evidence collection by the candidate may include naturally occurring situations, pre-set simulations, tests or questioning. (For an example of an assessment plan see Figure 8 below).

Your own evidence for unit D32, judging the performance of candidates, should include:

86

- the requirements for the evidence to be assessed

- strategy to show how it will be collected efficiently

- how you demonstrated that your assessment decisions were fair and that you provided appropriate feedback

It is important that candidates are given clear advice and encouragement about collecting their evidence for the elements or units in which they are being assessed.

Considerations here include:

- ensuring that candidates are aware of the requirements as set out in the standards for their award

- ease of access to such evidence

- negotiating appropriate work-based performances which best demonstrate your candidates' skills and knowledge.

- ensure that only the performance criteria identified in the elements are assessed. (These will normally be based on a professional judgement of competence).

Fig. 8: An example of an assessment plan

ASSESSMENT PLAN

QUALIFICATION: _____ UNIT NO: _____

ELEMENTS TO BE ASSESSED:

Element No.   Element Title

Methods of Assessment:

[ ]   Natural Performance   [ ]   Projects & Assignments   [ ]   Judgement of
                                                                                       other assessors
[ ]   Simulations   [ ]   Questioning

[ ]   Candidate & Peer Reports   [ ]   Candidate Prior Experience

Evidence to be collected

Assessment will take place:

Date: Time: Location:

Assessment Feedback:

Assessment agreement:

Assessor _____ Date _____   Candidate _____ Date _____

Name:_____   Name: _____

(I have briefed the candidate on the assessment, contents and appeals procedure)   (I agree with the assessment plan and am aware of the appeals procedure)

C&G7281/wn

Fig. 9: An example of an observation report

OBSERVATION REPORT

QUALIFICATION: _____

UNIT NO: _____ ELEMENT NO: _____

FEEDBACK ON OBSERVED ASSESSMENT	P.C.s, Range and Knowledge

Candidate Signature _____ Date _____

Assessor Signature _____ Date _____

DoncCollege/wn/99

88

Fig 10: An example of an assessor question report

ASSESSOR QUESTIONING REPORT

COURSE TITLE _____

P.C.s, Range and Knowledge	FEEDBACK FROM CANDIDATE

Candidate Signature _____ Date _____

Assessor Signature _____ Date _____

DoncCollege/wn/99

- ensuring that the evidence presented is both valid and authentic

- assessing against the performance criteria stated for the particular competence

- ensuring that the evidence is sufficient to demonstrate competence, is current and reflects the candidates' present abilities

- ensuring that the knowledge skills of the particular occupation are identified, and that issues concerning equal opportunities and the candidates individual needs are addressed.

You should remain unobtrusive during the assessment and should not interrupt your candidates' performance. Your candidates should be given feedback and advice afterwards if necessary. (See example Observation Report, Figure 9 below)

Your evidence to demonstrate your competence when collecting and assessing a candidate's knowledge through examination of products, observation, or responses to oral or written questioning, must show:

- the relevance of the evidence you have collected judged against the requirements of the element

- the validity of the evidence

- the fairness and reliability of the assessment process

- the quality of feedback provided to the candidate

A candidate's occupational knowledge may be used to support and enhance performance evidence. As with performance evidence, it is vital that knowledge evidence is judged against the knowledge specifications laid down in the occupational standards as well as the relevant performance criteria.

Questioning a candidate's knowledge should be done with sensitivity and in a way that is appropriate for their personality, confidence and experience. Such questioning may be either verbal or written, pre-set or devised by the assessor, and may conform to either the open or the closed questioning format (See example Questioning Report at Figure 10.)

To demonstrate your skills in making assessment decisions and giving feedback to a candidate your portfolio must:

- relate to the production of a record of assessment for one candidate covering at least three elements of competence

- show the way in which you provide feedback to the candidate being assessed

- show how you would provide feedback when there is insufficient evidence to demonstrate the candidate's competence

- include documentation recording the assessment: this must be legible and must meet both internal and external verification requirements

- show that you understand the need for secure document storage

- show that you are familiar with the accreditation process for the qualification

All assessment feedback should be recorded and agreed with the candidate, and you should sign and date the document. The feedback might be formative or summative. A formative assessment would be recorded on an assessment feedback document (See Figure 11 below). Summative assessments are usually recorded in the awarding body's record of assessment booklet, which should be signed and dated when the candidate has proved competence for the unit(s) being assessed.

Knowledge Evidence

Your evidence for unit D32 requires you to demonstrate your knowledge of the NVQ assessment process and the needs of candidates. You might include knowledge about:

- ways of involving candidates in the planning of assessments and in feedback sessions

- to identifying ways of evidence requirements

- the importance of work-based assessments and of different evidence collection methods

- when to use simulations and tests and how to administer them

- how candidates can gather knowledge evidence from different sources

- how to ensure candidates have access to fair and reliable assessments in line with equal opportunities and anti-discriminatory practice

- special assessment requirements and different levels of confidence and experience

- the importance of making fair and reliable assessment judgements against the standards

- how to remain unobtrusive during assessment of candidate's performance

- the reasons for good recording systems and subsequent verification processes

- how to deal with difficulties encountered during the assessment process, and where to obtain assistance

92

D33: Assess candidate using differing sources of evidence

Unit D33 relates to the collection and judgement of evidence from a variety of sources. These sources may include the candidate, the candidate's peers and others, the assessment of prior achievement (APA) and the outcomes of performance assessment covered in Unit D32. The main source of this evidence should be obtained from assessments of real work carried out by the candidate, although simulations can be used when appropriate.

This unit has three elements. These are concerned with:

- Agreeing and reviewing an assessment plan

- Judging evidence and providing feedback to candidates

- Making assessment decisions using differing sources of evidence and providing feedback to candidates

Fig. 11: An example of an assessor feedback sheet

| ASSESSMENT FEEDBACK SHEET |

Name of Candidate: _____

Qualification: _____

Unit No: _____   Element No(s): _____

FEEDBACK COMMENTS:

ACTION AGREED:

Candidate Signature _____ Date _____

Assessor Signature _____ Date _____

DonCollege/wn/99

93

The evidence requirements for this unit can be generated from your work for Unit D32 with additional evidence from further assessment opportunities. It is important that you experienced and inexperienced candidates to show your competence in assessing candidates with different degrees of confidence. You should demonstrate your ability to identify candidates with special assessment needs and to offer support to ensure that such candidates are fairly and reliably assessed.

Performance criteria

The performance criteria for D33 relate to:

* agreeing and reviewing three plans to assess candidates' competence. Each plan should refer to at least two elements and three sources of evidence (See Figure 11)

* judging various different sources of evidence derived from real performance, simulations, projects and assignments, questioning, candidate and peer reports, candidate prior achievement and learning. At least six judgements should be made from three or more different sources

* Making assessment decisions from the sources of evidence identified, relating to at least two elements of competence, and being able to demonstrate your competence at providing feedback.

Your evidence when agreeing and reviewing plans to assess candidates' performance should include the following points:

* the name of the qualification to be assessed

* the title of the unit and elements to be assessed

* selection evaluation of the different sources of evidence

* ways of ensuring the evidence is authentic, reliable and sufficient

* the location, time and date of the assessment

* any special facilities needed

* a date for reviewing the plan

94

- details of others who should be consulted

- assessor and candidate signatures with dates, to confirm the plan was agreed

- how disagreements during the planning process were dealt with

To demonstrate your skills when judging evidence and providing feedback to candidates, your portfolio should include:

- the evidence required for the to be assessment

- the efficiency of its collection

- the accuracy of your assessment decisions and

- the fairness of assessments and the quality of your feedback

Considerations here include:

- being aware of the differing needs of candidates: whether they are experienced, inexperienced or have special assessment requirements

95

- encouraging candidates to collect evidence to confirm their competence and knowledge from different sources

- showing how you check that evidence from prior achievement or learning is current and valid and meets the standards

- ensuring that candidates are aware of the requirement as set out in the standards for their award

- ease of access to ensuring they have evidence meeting those requirements

- ensuring that only the performance criteria identified in the elements are assessed. (These will normally be based on a professional judgement of competence.)

- the evidence presented is both valid and authentic.

- assessing against the performance criteria stated for the particular competence

- ensuring that the evidence is sufficient to demonstrate competence is current and reflects the candidates' present abilities

- explaining the guidelines you use to provide clear, constructive feedback to candidates with different needs both formally and informally

You should remain unobtrusive during the assessment and not interrupt your candidate's performance. The candidates should be given feedback and advice afterwards if necessary. (See example Observation Report, Fig. 9). During the assessment it may be appropriate to ask questions to confirm understanding: these should be recorded on an appropriate document. (See example Questioning Report, Fig. 10).

To demonstrate your skills in making assessment decisions using differing sources of evidence and in providing feedback to candidates your portfolio must meet the criteria listed on page 86.

96 The assessment of NVQ portfolios could provide valuable evidence for this unit. All assessment feedback should be recorded and agreed with the candidate, and you should sign and date the document. The feedback might be formative or summative. A formative assessment would be recorded on an assessment feedback document (See Fig.11). Summative assessments are usually recorded in the awarding body's record of assessment booklet, which should be signed and dated when the candidate has proved competence for the unit(s) being assessed.

Knowledge Evidence

Your evidence for unit D33 requires you to demonstrate your knowledge of the NVQ assessment process and the needs of candidates. You might include knowledge about:

- how to ensure candidates have access to fair and reliable assessments in line with equal opportunities and anti-discriminatory practice

- how to select opportunities and sources of evidence that are relevant to the assessment being made

- ways of involving candidates in the planning of assessments and in feedback sessions

- special assessment requirements and different levels of confidence and experience

- how to encourage candidates to be actively involved in their assessment without inhibiting them

- how to identify evidence requirements

- different sources and ways of collecting evidence

- when to use simulations and tests and how to administer them

- the importance of making fair and reliable assessment judgements against the standards

- how to give constructive feedback and advice to candidates with different levels of confidence and experience

- the reasons for good recording systems and subsequent verification processes

- how to deal with difficulties encountered during the assessment process, and where to obtain assistance.

Unit D36: Advise and support candidate to identify prior achievement

Unit D36 relates to those of you who are helping candidates to identify prior achievements for NVQ qualifications and to present evidence for assessment. This is not an assessor role, but an advisory one, in that you will not be making judgements but will be helping candidates to identify sources of evidence. However, to enable you to carry out this role, you will need to understand the national system of assessment and certification. As an Accreditation of Prior Learning (APL) advisor, you may be helping candidates to decide which qualification to aim for, in view of their prior experience and the available evidence.

As an adviser you will need to prove your competence in:

- helping candidates to identify relevant achievements

- preparing, agreeing and reviewing action plans for achieving qualifications

- helping candidates to prepare and present evidence for assessment

Candidates may be

- young or mature,

- employed or unemployed, or they may have

- special assessment requirements, or various different

- levels of confidence.

Performance Criteria

The performance criteria for unit D36 relate to:

- the way you give advice and support to identify areas of competence and achievement

- the interviewing of candidates and preparation of action plans

- the completion of records during the advice sessions

98

Your evidence when helping candidates to identify relevant achievements should show that you have:

- helped two candidates to identify relevant achievements.

- explained the processes involved in presenting evidence from prior experience.

- supported and encouraged candidates to review all relevant experience to identify possible qualification aims while maintaining their confidence and self-esteem. This should be observed by an assessor or supported by video or audiotape evidence.

Possible sources of evidence of prior experience, should include paid work, unpaid work, leisure activities, education and training.

Your evidence for agreeing and reviewing an action plan for achieving the selected qualification should include:

- an account of how you provided advice and encouragement, gathered evidence of prior achievement and suggested potential opportunities

- a description of the requirements for the qualification selected and the value of the evidence of prior achievement which has been identified

- notes of discussions with the candidates outlining the advice given and identifying which units/elements could be achieved through prior learning

- an explanation of how you helped candidates to maintain motivation and self-confidence. This could be supported by a statement from a candidate

- an agreed plan clearly identifying realistic actions and time scales, covering at least three elements of competence, and with arrangements for review

When helping candidates to collect and present evidence for assessment you need to:

- describe how evidence should be presented in a is well-structured portfolio with a clear referencing system

- make arrangements with assessors to review the portfolio with the candidate

- be aware of other sources of evidence that the candidate may use if prior achievement is not available

- understand the awarding body's requirements for documentation, evidence recording and procedures

Additionally, during your discussions with candidates, you need know of other options available to them if they disagree with the advice offered.

Knowledge Evidence

Your evidence for unit D36 should show you have knowledge of how to support and advise different candidates presenting evidence of prior achievement. This might include knowledge about:

- adapting your advice and support to meet the candidates' needs

- the types of information required from candidates to prove prior achievement and competence meeting national standards

- the appeals procedure to be used in cases of disagreement with your advice

- the system of NVQs, how to access various sources and the awards that may be obtained

- procedure for clarifying and analysing prior achievements

- the different ways of collecting evidence

- preparing action plans and encouraging candidates

- barriers to fair assessment and how to overcome them

- needs of candidates with different levels of experience and confidence or with special assessment requirements

100
- the assessment process and the preparation and structure of portfolios of evidence

UNDERPINNING KNOWLEDGE

The underpinning knowledge for the D units deals with your understanding of the assessment process. Your portfolio of evidence must show your knowledge of reliability, validity and fairness, approaches to assessment, and the framework for assessment.

Reliability, validity and fairness

Reliability relates to the consistency of assessment. Firstly it may be concerned with the consistency of judgments made by an assessor on different occasions when presented with the same evidence. Secondly, it may relate to the consistency of different assessors presented with the same evidence, and thirdly, to the consistent use of different assessment instruments when assessing the same competence. Jessop (1991) argues that reliability typically relates to a norm-referenced approach. Where the emphasis is on comparing individuals rather than focusing specific objectives or standards that is a more criterion-referenced approach.

Validity relates to the extent to which assessment instruments actually measure what they claim to. Jessop (1991) argues that this is an important component of the process as it uses external criteria: in the case of the NVQ process these criteria are the national standards of competence.

You must also show that the assessment was conducted under conditions which were fair. You should show your awareness of the need to allow candidates enough time to display their knowledge and skills, and that you know how to deal with the needs of candidates with special assessment requirements: time allowed for candidate feedback could be an important factor here.

To achieve fair assessment, it is important that

- the planning was negotiated with the candidates,

- with an agreement was needed about the timing of the assessment,

- agreement was reached about the place where the assessment would take place and the procedures that would be used

- the candidates were made aware of their rights

- agreement was reached about the element(s) of competence to be assessed and the types of evidence that would be considered.

Your plan should also include the method of assessment to be used and the arrangements made to review progress,and should set personal developmental targets for candidates.

There are two other requirements you need to take into account when considering evidence. These are its **sufficiency** and its **currency**. The concept of sufficiency relates to the quality of the evidence presented with respect to standards required: not only the standards for each element of competence but also those defined by the **Range Statements**. Range Statements are criteria which identify the framework within which the competence is set. Currency relates to the age of the evidence being presented: current evidence should be recent, and certainly not more than two years old.

Approaches to assessment

You need to make clear in your evidence that the approach to assessment you have used is only one of the many available, for example:

- standardised tests such as published reading tests

- checklists of skills

- profiles of attainment

- process or product related assessment

- observations of performance

- written records

- projects essays or assignments

- simulations or pre-set tests

- informal, teacher assessment led

- end-of-course examinations

- continuous assessment

The framework for assessment

Simulations

Where real evidence cannot be collected it may be necessary to use a simulation, where artificial conditions are set up to assess the candidate and you have to simulate the activity that is being assessed. If you have used this approach you should indicate this in your evidence. It is also important to show your knowledge of how such situations should be conducted.

102

Special assessment requirements

These can vary widely and might include emotional and social difficulties as well as medical and learning difficulties. Medical difficulties include hearing and sight problems while learning difficulties include literacy or numeracy problems. Your evidence should show how you have dealt with such situations or strategies you might use if they occurred.

Assessment decisions

Your portfolio show how, as an assessor, you were receptive to the needs of candidates, and should demonstrate abilities such as good planning, recording, communication and listening skills.

Feedback

Providing clear and constructive feedback to candidates is a key part of the assessment process. Feedback may be either verbal or written, and it is important that you take the level of self-confidence of the candidate into account when providing it.

There should be evidence that a summary of the assessment has **103** been provided for the candidates' use. Overall, the assessment process should be positive and encouraging for candidates, particularly where targets have not been achieved and further assessment is needed.

Types of evidence

There are two ways of collecting portfolio evidence. The best way is through the collection of **direct evidence** from performance, observations and questioning about what is being done. Other ways in which direct evidence can be provided is by using taped video or audio recordings or photographs.

Indirect evidence may be written testimonials, references or witness statements about levels of competence, and may be written by peers, line managers or the candidates themselves. Some candidates find a curriculum vitae (CV) can also be a useful source of evidence.

Other examples of indirect evidence include:

- minutes of meetings you have attended

- reports of activities

- certificates personal attainment

- records of appraisals

- information relating to professional competence and the use of systems which confirm previous experience and learning

Administration

The portfolio should reflect your responsibility as assessor for ensuring that the assessment session is administered appropriately and professionally. You must focus on the elements to be assessed and ensure that digressions are avoided as much as possible.

CASE STUDIES

Here is a collection of case studies taken from learners who have successfully completed their D units.

Unit D11

Malcolm is tutor and assessor of a City and Guilds computer-aided design vocational course, which includes the requirement for students to demonstrate practical skills. His evidence of assessing these skills for this unit

- two action plans agreed with learners, including the identification of relevant prior experience

- a chart indicating progress and skills achieved

- an explanation of how evidence was collected and monitored

- records of guidance provided during individual tutorial sessions with students, signed and dated by Malcolm and his students to confirm agreement

- feedback documentation completed when assignments were marked

- an explanation of course criteria and the marking and assessment scheme used

- records of assessment feedback and progress towards achievement of key skills from other assessors

- a rationale for the types of assessments and the techniques he used, including the method used for giving feedback

- an observation of assessment report confirming his competence in assessing an individual and providing feedback

- a report of questions asked by the assessor to confirm Malcolms underpinning knowledge

- assessment review sheets for two individuals providing feedback on progress

Unit D21

Sandra is a tutor in the prison service giving instruction for a City and Guilds number power qualification to prisoners. She gathered evidence for this unit from assessments she conducted, which included applying number skills and measuring. She selected two candidates being assessed for different units. For her evidence for this unit she collected:

105

- examples of assessment tasks designed to meet the requirements of the units she is assessing

- copies of assessment agreements completed with candidates which identify whether they have acquired the necessary skills and are ready for assessment

- examples of tasks completed by the candidates, which she has marked.

- assessment feedback documents completed when the tasks were done, identifying, by (using tick boxes) whether the criteria for the element were met.

- a record of Sandra's questioning to test the underpinning knowledge for the units.

- records of oral feedback which Sandra provided to candidates during one-to-one tutorial sessions

- completed copies of record sheets from the number power Personal Achievement Record, to confirm the assessment decision

- a rationale for the way Sandra conducted, explaining assessments and the skills she used to encourage her candidates to achieve. She identified their needs (who all have special assessment requirements), and addressed issues of security and confidentiality

- details of prison procedures relating to legal requirements, equal opportunities, and anti-discriminatory practice

Unit D32

Karen is a lecturer in the hairdressing salon at a further education college. She is responsible for delivering training and assessing NVQs in hairdressing for young adults. Her evidence for this unit included the following documentation:

- a statement prepared by Karen outlining her experience as a hairdresser, with copies of relevant certificates.

- an assessment plan covering one Level 2 NVQ unit

- consisting of three elements of competence. The plan was

- completed with the candidates, and signed and dated by them and Karen

- a statement about her candidates' experience and levels of confidence.

- a statement from the candidates giving authority for Karen to use documentation from her assessments as evidence for this unit

- written questions on the appeals procedure, answered by the candidates to confirm their understanding

- an observation checklist identifying which performance criteria and range and knowledge requirements Karen was able to assess. This included feedback given to candidates after assessment, agreed by signing and dating the checklist

- a list of oral questions asked during the assessment, with answers, signed and dated by the candidates and by Karen

- an assessment feedback document outlining how standards have been met and identifying areas where further assessment or training is required

- copies of summative assessment forms from the candidate pack, confirming assessment of competence where appropriate

- a report completed by Karen's assessor during an observation of an assessment conducted by her, together with questions asked

- a statement explaining how Karen conducts simulations if required

- A knowledge checklist completed by Karen showing she has met all the performance criteria and range and knowledge requirements of this unit

107

Unit D33

Dawn is a training co-ordinator responsible for candidates undertaking an NVQ in customer service. The candidates are employed in a number of different organisations and Dawn has the support of qualified work-based assessors. The candidates attend two weekly training sessions and Dawn is responsible for providing training, portfolio guidance and assessment. Her portfolio included:

- a copy of her CV

- three assessment plans, each covering a minimum of two elements and identifying at least three sources of evidence, signed and dated by the candidates and by Dawn. (One of these was cross-referenced with Unit D32)

- a statement describing the candidate profiles within the range of units to be assessed

- a report from an assessor who observed Dawn providing candidates with guidance on evidence collection

- records of portfolio guidance sheets completed by Dawn and agreed with the candidates

- feedback documentation from portfolio assessments. The evidence assessed included observation checklists completed by the work-based assessors, testimonial statements from work colleagues, assignments completed during training sessions, observation of simulated activities, oral and written questioning and a unit accreditation from the NVQ in Administration

- copies of candidates' summary of evidence sheets from the candidate pack

- supplementary statements prepared by Dawn to support the performance criteria and range requirements of this unit.

- a knowledge checklist completed by Dawn

Unit D36

108

Janice is a tutor in the Department of Business Studies and Office Technology in a college. She teaches the NVQ in Administration at NVQ Levels 2 and 3. She has selected two candidates: one is a mature employed adult who has a confident personality and is working for the Level 3 qualification; the other is young and unemployed and is working for Level 2. Both candidates have prior achievement they can count towards their qualifications. Janice included the following evidence in her portfolio:

- a candidate APL guidance booklet

- a form completed with Janice's candidates, containing personal details,

- a statement completed by each candidate describing employment history, training and education experience or learning they wish to have accredited

- a summary of guidance given by Janice during interviews with her candidates

- copies of the relevant awarding body criteria being used

- statements completed by candidates confirming that guidance provided was supportive and motivated them

- an audio tape of interviews with the two candidates

- details of the college's appeals procedure

- copies of two action plans Janice has agreed with her candidates

- notes on reviews carried out during evidence collection

- copies of Unit Summary Record pages from the candidates' Cumulative Assessment Record. This lists the evidence of prior achievement, and how the performance criteria have been met. Janice has highlighted the APL evidence to match it with other evidence supporting prior achievement claims.

- feedback reports from the assessors who assessed the candidates' portfolios

REFERENCE TO OTHER UNITS   109

The evidence you have collected for units D11 and D21, themselves linked, may also be usefully cross-referenced with other elements:

A222   'Identify learning needs with individuals'

C212   'Support learners needs'

C222   'Review learning programmes and agree modifications with learners'

E231   'Collect and analyse information on training and development sessions'

There is a great deal of cross-referencing of evidence between units D32 and D33, and evidence relating to planning and review may be inter-linked with unit D36.

SUMMARY

This chapter has detailed the requirements for a portfolio of evidence for the D units. The five units described in this chapter cover both NVQ-type assessments and those following a more traditional approach. Units D32, D33 and D36 are mutually exclusive and appropriate for NVQ-type assessments only, while units D11 and D21 are suitable for other approaches to assessment.

110

CHAPTER SEVEN

The E Units
Evaluation

Introduction

The City and Guilds E units focus on the evaluation and assessment of your own practice, both personal and professional. The chapter includes two important strands. The first is a personal reflection on your own performance to aid future planning. The second concentrates on meeting professional requirements both through changes in the curriculum in your own subject area and through national policy and legislation changes affecting the delivery of further and adult education. Particular attention will be paid to the following issues:

- appropriate sources of evidence on which to draw when evaluating your own practice

- methods of reflecting on your own experiences and those of your learners

- likely sources of professional support

- the influence of your own values, beliefs and life experiences on your teaching

- current issues and trends within further and adult education

- likely future developments in further and adult education

At NVQ Level 3 there are three units on offer. These are E23 Evaluate training and development sessions, E31 Evaluate and develop own practice and E32 Managing relations with colleagues and customers. The focus of unit E23 relates to evaluating your own teaching or training sessions, while E31 is concerned with the evaluating and developing your own practice in response to changes that might have occurred outside your classroom. Unit E32 relates to working effectively with colleagues and customers with whom you come into contact as a teacher or trainer.

PORTFOLIO REQUIREMENTS

E23: Evaluate training and development sessions

Unit E23 comprises two elements: E231, which is concerned with the collection and analysis of information about your training and development sessions and E232, which focuses on how you might attempt to make improvements to your professional skills. E23 is concerned with improving the effectiveness of your teaching skills in a structured way. The performance criteria for this unit, suggest that this process should be cyclical, ongoing throughout your work, and may be either informal or formal. For this unit it is best if the evaluation is formal: the use of teaching sessions you have formally evaluated will generally make your job of evidence collection easier.

112 The focus for the collection of evidence is twofold. Firstly, you need to demonstrate how you actively selected an appropriate evaluation strategy that provided you with accurate information from your learners. Secondly, the evidence in your portfolio should indicate improvements to your practice resulting from an analysis of the information you collected. With this in mind, your evidence for this unit may be cross-referenced with evidence for other units, particularly the C units,

Your portfolio for Unit E23 may include information on:

- national or organisational standards, and changes in national or European Union (EU) legislation that have impacted on your practice

- changes in your training or teaching methods, the management and content of your sessions or the use of resources

Performance Criteria

The performance criteria for unit E23 are concerned with the following:

- how you selected a suitable teaching or training session to meet the requirements of this unit

- how you organised your evaluation of the session. (You should consider doing this by selecting an appropriate methodology to collect and analyse data from as wide a range of sources as possible)

- how you set your learners at ease when collecting this information

- the method of collecting the evidence, the clarity and relevance of your questions and the need for confidentiality and anonymity

- how you gained approval of colleagues for your chosen methodology

- methods you used to analyse the data you collected. (You should show that all your available data has been analysed)

- decisions you took towards improving your teaching. (Your evidence should show that these improvements were realistic and were initiated without delay)

- your approach to drawing up a plan setting out your personal objectives for introducing developments. (This plan should not only take into account feasibility and potential benefit to your learners, but should also show that you had the agreement of the appropriate people in your workplace)

- the production of a report to show how these improvements were effectively introduced

- instances (if appropriate) of how you repeated the process outlined above for other sessions you conducted

113

Knowledge Evidence

The knowledge evidence for this unit requires you to be aware of:

- the various methods available for evaluating sessions with your learners

- how to identify the criteria for your evaluation

- how to collect information effectively and efficiently from your learners and others

- approaches to improvement in the wider field of adult education and training

- how to make improvements to your sessions

- factors that might influence the successful introduction of change

- the requirements of employment and equal opportunities legislation and good practice

- national and organisational debates relating to the development of adult education and training

E31: Evaluate and develop own practice

Unit E31 is composed of three elements. E311 is concerned with evaluating your own practice, E312 with identifying your own self-development needs and setting personal targets, and E313 with adapting your practice to meet targets you have set for yourself. The unit focuses on the extent to which you have met your professional self-improvement goals. Like Unit E23, this unit concentrates on collecting evidence from various sources in order to make judgements about your professional practice. In this unit, however, the focus of attention is on influences from outside your classroom.

The evidence you need to complete this unit should come from your own evaluations of your performance in the classroom or workshop, and should show the impact of changes you have made as a result of reports, research and national legislation in the area of adult education and training. It should show that you are keeping up-to-date with developments and changes in your own area of teaching or training, and that you are aware of changes in other similar areas.

You should consider the collection of evidence for this unit in two stages, the **preparation stage** and the **implementation** stage. The preparation stage is concerned with an analysis of your individual needs and with planning your activities, and covers the requirements of E311. The implementation stage focuses on elements E312 and E313, and concentrates on the implementation of changes to improve your practice, and a review of their impact on both your learners and your colleagues.

Performance Criteria

To meet the performance criteria for this unit you should provide evidence that you have:

- assessed the standards used to evaluate your work. These standards should be clearly stated in your evidence and must be appropriate for your work, realistic and achievable. Your evidence needs to show that you have spent some time **115** evaluating your practice and identifying your targets in the light of reports or changes in legislation reflecting the changes you wish to make. Targets should be clear and realistic, based on an accurate assessment of all the information, and should be set in conjunction with others who work with you.

- gathered evidence of your own performance in relation to these goals and targets. When collecting your evidence you should ensure that the process you have used is both realistic and valid

- identified ways of achieving targets you have not yet met. In meeting this objective you should consider the impact the changes might have on others, and should take into consideration the views of your colleagues. As a result of your analysis, you should draw up a personal action plan to meet your targets

- analysed all the evidence and matched it against your targets

- revised you targets in the light of the evidence

- produced a report reflecting the approach that you used and indicating the results of your activities

Knowledge Evidence

Your knowledge evidence for unit E31 should demonstrate your understanding of the following:

- methods of self assessment

- approaches towards prioritising your personal self-development needs

- how to produce a personal action plan

- who to ask for help in analysing and interpreting evidence about your performance

- personal and organisational needs

- government policy affecting your work

- current debates about adult education and training, and how these affect your practice

- how to promote change effectively in an organisation

E32: Managing relations with colleagues and customers

Unit E32 has two elements, E321 Managing relationships with colleagues and E322 Managing relationships with customers. The unit concentrates on your work with other members of your organisation and those outside it with whom you have professional contact

The evidence you present should demonstrate your professional skills when working as part of a team, and may be drawn from either regular or occasional contacts. Regular contacts might include colleagues, support staff or your line manager and customers, while occasional contacts might include external veri-

116

fiers, employers, parents or training officers from local companies.

Performance Evidence

To meet the performance criteria for unit E32, you need to show that you:

- establish and maintain honest and professional relationships with colleagues and customers

- seek support from an appropriate person if difficulties arise with colleagues or customers

- share information, opinions and advice with others, and where there is a difference of views you resolve it in a professional manner. Your portfolio should show that you encourage colleagues to feel comfortable to expressing their views, and that you ask for help in a way that will not give offence

- are sensitive when offering your colleagues and customers help and advice or when deciding how to allocate work among colleagues. When dealing with colleagues, you should take account of their complementary skills, knowledge, experience and personal development needs

117

Knowledge evidence

Your knowledge evidence for E32 should demonstrate your understanding of:

- factors that aid the building of meaningful relationships with adults

- sources of support available to help you to deal with colleagues and customers who present difficulties

- differences in cultural and personal values that can affect relationships with colleagues and customers

- approaches for offering advice to colleagues taking into account their individual needs and characteristics

- current equal opportunities and anti-discriminatory practice

UNDERPINNING KNOWLEDGE

The underpinning knowledge for the E units relates to:

- evaluating your own teaching,

- external factors that might influence the change

- influences on making change

- managing your relationships

Evaluating your own teaching

Your portfolio should indicate that you are aware of the importance of evaluating the quality of your teaching. This is one of the most important ways of developing your professional skills, and the informal, personal approach to evaluation is often part of a natural process of self-inspection.

You should demonstrate your awareness of collecting data about your teaching. There are a number of ways you might tackle this. Reece and Walker (1997) identified four possible approaches:

118

- personal reflection

- classroom and mini-teaching observations by your colleagues

- video recording your sessions

- ascertaining the views of your learners through the use of questionnaires or interviews

You should also show that you have considered the validity of your procedures for collecting your evidence. For example, your evidence might show that you have considered the following questions:

- Are your questions appropriate and clearly constructed?

- Have you worded them in a neutral way?

- Do they focus on the needs of the learners?

- Will they tell you what you need to know?

- Does the way you have presented them ensure confidentiality for those you have questioned?

Your portfolio should show that personal evaluation is a routine, ongoing process. Both the efficiency and effectiveness of your teaching sessions should be considered, as should external factors affecting what you teach and how you teach it. Your evaluations should be made against predetermined objectives and should take into account all the factors affecting your teaching. These include **planning, performance,** and **resource** issues.

- When evaluating **planning issues** you might include an evaluation of the organisation and structure of the sessions you teach. Issues you might consider include the length of the sessions, the timing and length of breaks, and the balance between the amount of subject knowledge and practical work and theory in your sessions.

- **Performance issues** relate to your work in the classroom. You might include here an analysis of level of work you are presenting to your learners and the pace at which you are introducing it, the level of motivation and enthusiasm, and the feedback you receive. Other considerations might include your questioning and listening skills, or your effectiveness at introducing or ending sessions.

119

- To evaluate **resource issues** you might focus on the type and purpose of the resources you use, their appropriateness for your learners, their clarity, your level of dependency on them and their cost-effectiveness.

Other issues you should consider here include the recruitment and retention of your learners, your inter-personal skills, the cost-effectiveness of your programme and the quality of knowledge and skills your sessions have provided.

External factors that might influence change

Changes in government policy, national legislation and international law as well as changes in social and economic circumstances all help to ensure that the education and training of adults is subject to constant change. The E units are concerned with your ability to recognise and accept the need for change in your workplace as well as actively promoting it. Your portfolio should show that you have considered these sources of change.

Underpinning knowledge for unit E31 relates particularly to three issues. These are **sources of potential change** that may affect your work, **strategies to promote change** and an understanding of your **own attitude** towards change.

Sources of potential change

It is an important part of this unit that you demonstrate your awareness of the sources of change that may affect your work as a teacher or trainer. These sources are both internal and external to your job and affect not only what you teach but also how you do it. It is important that you show not only the sources of change but also the sources of information which will keep you up to date. These include journals, newspapers and magazines produced for those who work in your specialist area, as well as other media such as the Times Educational Supplement, The Guardian, educational journals, literature produced by relevant trade unions, and television and radio programmes. Your evidence for this unit should indicate not only that you have kept yourself up-to-date but also how you have achieved this.

120

Managing relationships

The E units expect that you will have spent time evaluating your professional relationship with learners, colleagues and others you come into contact with as part of your work. When doing this you will need to consider:

- your own values and beliefs, which may not necessarily co-incide with those of others, for example over equal opportunities or anti-discriminatory policies

- the age of those with whom you are dealing and their role within their organisation

- the socio-economic status and individual value systems of those with whom you are working. (Differences here may help you, for example, to account for discrepancies in levels of vocabulary or a lack of understanding of your specialist jargon)

- cultural and ethnic differences of those who come to your sessions. (These can lead to problems with religious or social issues, as well as cultural confusions such as the interpretation of body language)

CASE STUDIES

Here are some examples of evidence that has been collected by learners to complete their evidence for the E units.

Unit E23
Case study 1

Margaret is a lecturer in further education teaching community courses to adults. These are short courses, which are delivered each term and attract funding enabling the college to offer the courses free to specific sections of the community. For this unit she has gathered evidence about her evaluation of these courses, comprising:

- an evaluation plan outlining her reasons for evaluation and the method selected. This included the targets for her groups and the time available

121

- an example of the questionnaire used, with her evaluation criteria and a rationale for her method of collecting data

- a summary of the data collected

- an analysis of the data, identifying areas where she could make improvements for future courses

- a report making recommendations to her section head and justifying the proposed improvements. The recommendations included training methods, planning, resources and content

- minutes of course team meetings recording discussion of her evaluation findings

- a printout of the data collected from learners who completed the college Student Perception of Course form (SPOC). She prepared a report to help identify any improvements

- a self-evaluation logbook containing entries about her perception of selected sessions throughout the duration of her course

- supplementary information relating to national debates and changes in education, training and development

Case study 2

A training company employs Tony as a trainer for Health and Safety and First Aid courses. He delivers training courses to employees of mainly large production companies around the country. This is a competitive area and to maintain the training contracts he needs to ensure his training is of the highest standard and provides value for money. His evidence for E23 included:

- an evaluation plan outlining areas of his training which need to be closely monitored, and his justification for the methods used

- examples of questionnaires completed by participants in two of his training courses

122

- an explanation of the criteria against which he is evaluating, with reference to performance indicators, national standards and organisational standards

- Tony's analysis of the feedback from the two sets of questionnaires, identifying areas he could improve

- examples of questionnaires completed by managers of the companies to determine their satisfaction with the courses offered

- a selection of letters from companies which have been satisfied with the training Tony has provided. These commented on specific aspects of the training and provided verbal feedback from employees

- a copy of a three-monthly report Tony prepares for his manager, identifying possible improvements to maintain the company's competitiveness and their feasibility

- a rationale for the selection of the evaluation methods and criteria used.

- evidence of his understanding of equal opportunities

- legislation and training and development issues.

Unit E31
Case study

Claire is an inexperienced tutor in further education and has completed her first year of teaching. The course she taught was an RSA CLAIT course for adults of differing ages and abilities who required varying levels of support. She conducted an extensive self-evaluation throughout the course and included the following evidence for this unit:

- a self-evaluation log with entries recording critical incidents for a selection of sessions

- a completed course evaluation document recording retention and achievement outcomes with self-assessment grading for different areas of the course

- copies of evaluation forms completed by her learners

- records of verbal evaluation sessions conducted with her learners at the end of each term

- a report including her analysis of the evaluation data collected from questionnaires, discussion and her self-evaluation log

- copies of witness testimonies obtained from her colleagues and a report from an external examiner on her standard of marking

- details of government policies and current debates relating to further education and proposed changes for her college

- copies of her college's mission statement and vision for the future, and of her department's strategic plan for the forthcoming academic year

- a review of her personal action plan prepared at the beginning of the course with details of future goals and targets, includ-

123

ing how she hopes to develop her own practice, and courses that would enable her to do this

- an explanation of forthcoming changes anticipated for her college and how she may be affected, stating her attitude to the changes

- reference to an assessment of observed teaching sessions

- details of an appraisal with her line manager, including her input and feedback from the appraiser

REFERENCE TO OTHER UNITS

Evidence you have collected for this unit may be suitably cross-referenced with other relevant parts of the E Units, as well as the following Level 3 elements:

- A221 'Identify available learning opportunities'

- C213 'Promote access to learning and achievement'

- C214 'Promote anti-discriminatory practice'

- C222 'Review learning programmes and agree modifications with learners'

- D111 'Collect information on learners' progress'

- D113 'Review progress with learners'

- D331 'Review and agree an assessment plan'

and units:

- B21 'Design learning programmes to meet learners' requirements'

- C21 'Create a climate conducive to learning'

- C23 'Facilitate learning in groups through presentation and activities'

- C24 'Facilitate learning through demonstration and instruction'

- C27 'Facilitate group learning'

- D11 'Monitor and review progress with learners'

SUMMARY

This chapter has described some of the important factors you should consider when putting together a portfolio of evidence for the E units. The performance criteria in this unit concentrate on your skills evaluating and developing your own practice. The underpinning knowledge suggests some of the factors you need to consider when making changes to your practice. These changes may arise either from your own evaluation of your practice as a result of national developments in your subject area, or legislative changes.

GLOSSARY

ACCESS: the opportunity for a learner to pursue an NVQ award, if they can demonstrate an appropriate level of competence.

ACCREDITATION: The formal approval by the Qualifications and curriculum Authority (QCA) for an Awarding Body to have their award included as part of the NVQ or SVQ framework.

ACCREDITATION OF PRIOR LEARNING (APL): Giving credit towards an NVQ award on the basis of evidence collected from past experience.

ASSESSMENT ACTION PLAN: A learner's plan for tackling a unit or part of a unit of competence

ASSESSMENT: The process of making judgements, against written criteria, based on evidence collected, about individual competence.

ASSESSEE: The person being assessed

ASSESSOR: The person making an assessment

AWARD: A term used to describe what the individual receives on achieving an NVQ.

AWARDING BODY: A group or organisation approved by QCA to provide NVQ awards.

CERTIFICATE: The document the learner receives from an Awarding Body. It provides evidence that the NVQ or units of competence have been achieved.

CERTIFICATION: The process of assessing, recording and formally issuing an award confirming competence to required standards.

CITY AND GUILDS: An Awarding Body, offering awards in a wide range of occupations, including training.

COMPETENCE: The ability to perform tasks to nationally agreed standards in working situations.

CORE KEY SKILLS: Basic skills that underpin competent performance across all vocational areas.

CORE UNITS: Mandatory units of competence that reflect required levels of core skills in specific occupations.

CREDIT ACCUMULATION: Building up, through a process of certification, units of competence over a period of time.

CREDIT TOWARDS: The attainment and recording of elements or units of competence, which may result in NVQ award

EDEXEL, EDUCATIONAL EXCELLENCE, formerly BUSINESS AND TECHNICAL EDUCATION COUNCIL (BTEC): An Awarding Body predominantly concerned with technical or occupational awards

ELEMENT/ELEMENT OF COMPETENCE: The smallest part of activity that can be credited towards the achievement of a unit of competence in an NVQ.

EVIDENCE: Anything that is presented by a learner as proof of competence.

128

EVIDENCE REQUIREMENTS: Evidence of performance and underpinning knowledge is required to successfully complete a unit

EXPERIENTIAL LEARNING: The acquisition of skills, knowledge and understanding through personal experience. This experience, in a number of different forms, can sometimes be put forward for award accreditation.

GENERIC UNITS: Units that form a compulsory part of an award, see also core units

KEY PURPOSE: A term agreed by the Lead Body, describing the occupation to which a specified set of standards applies.

KNOWLEDGE EVIDENCE: Evidence that demonstrates an understanding of a topic through wider reading or discussion

LEAD BODY: The body responsible for setting occupational standards. These groups are sometimes called Lead Industry Bodies (LIB) and are made up of employees, and professional advisers as well as employer representatives

LEARNING: In NVQ terms, the process of acquiring skill, knowledge and understanding contributing to occupational competence.

LOCAL ENTERPRISE COUNCIL (LEC): A body, mainly composed of local employers, appointed to instigate, monitor and support training initiatives in Scotland. Such bodies are similar to the Training and enterprise Councils (TECs) in England and Wales

LEVEL: A term used to describe degrees of competence, in relation to the complexity and responsibility attached to the occupation. There are five levels in the NVQ framework. All the units dealt with in this book are at NVQ Level 3

MANAGEMENT CHARTER INITIATIVE (MCI): The Lead Body responsible for the production of occupational standards for various levels of manager across employment areas.

MONITORING: The process of observing and checking an activity

NVQ CRITERIA: Relates to validity, consistency and reliability (see also Rules of Evidence)

NATIONAL RECORD OF ACHIEVEMENT (NRA): A learner's record of training and experience.

NATIONAL VOCATIONAL QUALIFICATION (NVQ): An award accredited by QCA, demonstrating competence in a given occupational area.

NVQ FRAMEWORK: A national system, which places individual NVQs into their appropriate occupations and level of competence within the overall NVQ framework.

OCCUPATIONAL AREAS: Categories of jobs with similar functions that require common areas of competence.

OPTIONAL UNITS: Units a learner is able to choose as part of an NVQ award.

OXFORD, CAMBRIDGE AND RSA (OCR): An Awarding Body, offering awards in a wide range of occupations.

PERFORMANCE CRITERIA: Criteria that set out levels of performance, and describe the activities relating to specific elements of competence to be demonstrated in each element or unit

PRIOR ACHIEVEMENT: Learning acquired in the past, which may not have been recorded (see also APEL above).

PROGRESSION: Movement through the NVQ framework either from one level to a higher level or across occupational boundaries.

PROVIDER/(TRAINING PROVIDERS): Organisation or employer with primary responsibility for providing appropriate training

QUALIFICATION: The formal recognition that the defined standard has been achieved.

QCA (QUALIFICATIONS AND CURRICULUM AUTHORITY): The body responsible for validating and accrediting standards for Awarding Bodies in England and Wales.

QUALITY ASSURANCE: Guarantee of the quality of an award being offered through an agreed process and monitoring and verifying the standard.

REVIEW: The process of checking that trainee progress is being enabled, and that no obstacles to learning exist.

130

RANGE STATEMENT: A statement which describes the range and context of activities within which a specified unit or element of competence applies.

ROYAL SOCIETY OF ARTS (RSA): An Awarding Body that offers awards in a number of areas, particularly those relating to information technology.

RULES of EVIDENCE: relating to the validity, authenticity, currency and sufficiency of evidence presented for assessment

SCOTTISH VOCATIONAL EDUCATION COUNCIL (SCOTVEC): The body responsible for the validation and accreditation of standards, awards and Awarding Bodies in Scotland.

SCOTTISH VOCATIONAL QUALIFICATION (SVQ): The equivalent, in Scotland, of the NVQ in England and Wales.

STANDARD: The measure of competence agreed by the Lead Body, which describes what has to be achieved to gain an element or unit of competence.

STATEMENT OF COMPETENCE: The format in which units and elements of competence are described identifying the activities required to ensure competence in given occupational areas.

TRAINING AND ENTERPRISE COUNCIL (TECs): A nationally based organisation of eighty-nine councils in England and Wales. (The Scottish equivalent are called Local Enterprise Councils (LECs)). These bodies have been given the responsibility for running the government-sponsored youth and adult training programmes.

TRAINING AND DEVELOPMENT LEAD BODY (TDLB): This Lead Body represents a cross-section of organisations and institutions in the training sphere. They are responsible for deciding standards for training and assessment.

TRAINING ENTERPRISE AND EDUCATION DIRECTORATE OF THE EMPLOYMENT DEPARTMENT (TEED): A Government body set up to monitor, support and/or fund relevant training initiatives, including the work of TECs and LECs.

UNIT: A quantity of work activity large enough to be of value to an employer. It is capable of certification independent and of constituting a credit towards an NVQ or SVQ award. It consists of a number of elements of competence.

131

VERIFICATION: The process of ensuring that the standard of assessment is being maintained, and that appropriate systems are in place to meet awarding body requirements.

VERIFIER: An individual appointed to ensure the maintenance of the NVQ Standard, ensuring that the Awarding Body's requirements are met. Verifiers may be internal, officers of the Approved Assessment Centre, or external, appointed by the Awarding Body.

References

Curzon, L. B. (1990, 4th Edn.) Teaching in Further Education: an Outline of Principles and Practice. London: Cassell

Daines, J., Daines, C. and Graham, B. (1993) Adult Learning, Adult Teaching Nottingham: University of Nottingham

FENTO (1999) Standards for Teaching and Supporting Learners in Further Education in England and Wales London: Further Education Training Organisation

Rutter, M. and Rutter M. (1992) Developing Minds: Challenge and Continuity Across the Lifespan London: Penguin

Reece, I. and Walker, S. (1997, 3rd Edn.) A Practical Guide to Teaching, Training and Learning Sunderland: Business Education Publishers

Stakes, J. R. and Hornby G. (1996) Meeting Special Needs in Mainstream Schools A Practical Guide for Teachers London David Fulton

Walkin, L. (1996) Training and Development NVQs Cheltenham: Stanley Thornes

133